DISCERNING YOUR SPIRITUAL JOURNEY WITH SAINT JOHN OF AVILA

DISCERNING YOUR SPIRITUAL JOURNEY WITH SAINT JOHN OF AVILA

DOCTOR OF THE CHURCH

DENISE CLARE OLIVER

GRACEWING

First published in 2013 by
Gracewing
2 Southern Avenue
Leominster
Herefordshire HR6 0QF
United Kingdom
www.gracewing.co.uk

ISBN 978 085244 766 6

Typeset by Gracewing

Cover design by Bernardita Peña Hurtado

I dedicate this book to
Pope Emeritus Benedict XVI

In thanksgiving for his Pontificate
and for his loving and humble dedication
and service to Christ and His Church

CONTENTS

Acknowledgements

I GIVE THANKS TO the Holy Spirit who inspired me with the idea for this book in St Peter's Square on the Solemnity of Pentecost in 2012.

This book owes a special thank you to Rev Dr Paul Haffner for his encouragement and kindness during the whole writing process of this book. An expression of gratitude is also due to Professor Christina Pal for her constant encouragement, and her helpful suggestions and editorial expertise in helping to improve this work. I am grateful to Fr Luke Buckles O.P. for being an inspiration as both a lecturer in theology, and mentor in the spiritual life. My thanks also go to my family for their love and encouragement whilst I was in the process of writing this book.

INTRODUCTION

'G OD SO LOVED the world that He gave His only Son...' (Jn 3:16). He sent His Son into the world so that we might have life and have it to the full (Jn 10:10). In the busy-ness of our lives, we may often find it difficult to set aside quiet time for reflection. Yet, if we can find a moment to stop, we recognise that we have a deep longing inside—a yearning to be fulfilled, to be happy and satisfied in our life. St Augustine once wrote, 'Our hearts are restless.' As we read these words of the great Father of the Church, they resonate deep within us. We may try many methods to satisfy that desire for happiness, but in the end we learn that our hearts are restless until they rest in the Lord; for He has made us for Himself, and only He can satisfy the deepest longing of our hearts. The Lord Jesus loves each one of us, and calls us to superabundant joy. He tells His disciples the secret to obtaining this joy. He says, 'Remain in me, as I remain in you... remain in my love... I have told you this so that my joy may be in you and your joy may be complete' (Jn 15:4, 9, 11). The Lord Jesus knocks at the door of our hearts continually; He wants us to know Him, to love Him, and to follow Him, for it is in following God's will that our true happiness lies.

The Lord has a unique calling for each one of us; no one's vocation is exactly the same. There are vocations to the priesthood, consecrated life, married life and single life; however, within these vocations, each person's mission and journey will be different. We have the blessing of the Saints whom we can imitate and follow, but God calls each of us to be the unique person He has created, and to fulfil the unique mission for which He has created us. Before He formed us in our mother's womb, He knew us (Jr 1:5), and He draws us as a loving Father to participate in His providential plan.

The word 'vocation' comes from the Latin *voco, vocare* meaning *to call*. To discern our vocation, we must walk by faith, following the Lord's lead, as He shows us—little by little—the direction for our lives. Throughout our journey, we hear many voices—the voices of secularism and materialism, the voices of a world always pressed for time, and even the voices of well-meaning friends and family. In discerning our vocation, we must strive to filter out the voices of the world so that we can hear the voice of the Good Shepherd, calling us to follow Him unreservedly; for He says to each one of us, 'It was not you who chose me, but I who chose you and appointed you to go and bear fruit that will remain,' (Jn 15:16).

The Lord Jesus calls each of us to remain in Him. To abide in Jesus is to experience a deep, intimate, personal union with Him. This is the path to personal fulfilment, interior peace, and lasting joy. This is our true calling and the goal of every vocation. If we follow the teaching of St John of Avila, we will have some basic tools to help us reach this deep and intimate relationship with the Lord. If we truly desire to do the will of God and remain faithful to the message of the Gospel, God will not let us miss the unique and specific calling which He has for us. As we grow in union with the Lord and as our lives become more and more rooted in Him, we learn to hear His voice more clearly and discern the path He has for us with greater certitude. The spiritual doctrine unfolded in the following chapters is not a list of guidelines on how to discern whether one is called to the priesthood, consecrated life, married life or single life; rather the goal of these chapters is to help us discern our spiritual journey toward union with the Lord.

On 7 October 2012, Pope Benedict XVI declared St John of Avila a Doctor of the Church, making him the thirty-fourth Saint to have been given this eminent title. St John of Avila is 'one of the most significant figures of the Catholic Reformation in Spain'.[1] However, until now he has not been widely known in the English speaking world. It is no coincidence that God has raised up St John of Avila to the title of Doctor of the Church in our time. His writings are particularly relevant for this Year of Faith, designated by Pope Benedict XVI on the fiftieth anniversary of the opening of the Second Vatican Council. St John of Avila's zeal for both living and spreading the message of the gospel is a perfect example for priests, religious, and laity desiring to live out their Christian life in deep communion with Christ. Fr Avila's book *Audi Filia*, provides us with solid information for understanding the richness of our Catholic Faith and the beauty of a soul that is in a state of grace. The fact that John of Avila was so grounded in Sacred Scripture and had such a passion for teaching the truth also makes him an 'outstanding precursor of the new evangelisation'.[2] When he was canonized on 31 May 1970, Pope Paul VI said that he is an 'advocate of ecclesiastical reform and stressed his continuing influence down to our own time'.[3]

Fr Avila believed that holy priests are essential to the renewal of the Church. He had constant concern for those aspiring to the priesthood; to this end he tirelessly worked towards moral and spiritual reform of the clergy and the instruction and education of 'boys and young men, especially those studying for the priesthood'.[4] Fr Avila was also well sought after by his contemporaries for spiritual direction and discernment. He helped all who came his way—beginners and proficients, saints and sinners, young and old.[5] In our time, we can also look to this great Saint and Doctor of the Church, to guide us through the challenges we face on our spiritual journey. Fr Avila is a Saint for all people and all times; in fact, Pope Benedict XVI refers to him as a 'pioneer in pointing to the universal call to holiness'.[6] He is a marvellous example, witness, and mentor for the new evangelisation.

St John of Avila was a gifted preacher, spiritual director, and confessor; his advice was drawn from experience, learning, and the gifts God had given him. During the years of his ministry, he became known as **the** 'Apostle of Andalusia' and '**Master**'. Among St John of Avila's disciples were St Teresa of Avila, St John of God, St Francis Borgia,[7] and Venerable Anne of the Cross.[8] Both John of God and Francis Borgia were converted as a consequence of hearing the powerful preaching of John of Avila, and Teresa of Avila, the great Saint and Doctor of the Church, had the account of her life and mystical experiences confirmed as authentic by Fr Avila. This account is what we know today as *The Book of Her Life*. Teresa of Avila, struggling as to whether her mystical experiences were authentic, was advised to write an account of her life so that she could send it to Fr Avila, because he was well known for his wise spiritual direction and his reputation for holiness. In a letter to Fr García de Toledo concerning this account she writes, 'I urgently desire that he be asked for his opinion about it since this was my intention in beginning to write. If it seems to him I am walking on a good path, I shall be very consoled; then nothing else would remain for me than to do what lies within my power.'[9]

Notes

1   Rady Roldan-Figueroa, 'Espirituación: Juan de Ávila's Doctrine of Union with the Holy Spirit' in *Renaissance and Reformation / Renaissance et Réforme* vol. XXIX / issue 2–3 (2005), p. 65.

2   Pope Benedict XVI, *Apostolic Letter Proclaiming Saint John of Avila, diocesan priest, a Doctor of the Universal Church* (Vatican City: Libreria Editrice Vaticana, 2012), 1. (Hereafter cited as *Apostolic Letter*.)

3   *Ibid.*

4   *Ibid.*, 2.

5   *Ibid.*, 7.

6   *Ibid.*, 6.

7   Anna Hamling, 'John of Avila' in *The Encyclopedia of Christian Literature*, edited by George Thomas Kurian & James D. Smith, III, vol. 1, Genres and Types/Biographies A-G (Lanham, MD: Scarecrow Press, Inc. 2010), p. 392.

8   Longaro degli Oddi, *Life of the Blessed Master John of Avila; Secular Priest, Called the Apostle of Andulusia* (London: Burns and Oates, 1898), p. 39.

9   Teresa of Avila, *The Book of Her Life* in *The Collected Works*, translated by Kieran Kavanaugh and Otilio Rodriguez (Washington, D.C.: Institute of Carmelite Studies, 1980), p. 364.

1

THE LIFE OF ST JOHN OF AVILA

OHN OF AVILA was born in the year 1499 or 1500 on 6 January, the feast of the Epiphany, at Almodóvar del Campo, in the Archdiocese of Toledo[1] to Alfonso Ávila and Catalina Gijón who were from good families and well-known for their piety.[2] John's parents, Alfonso and Catalina longed to have children, but after some years of marriage Catalina had still not conceived. She decided to undertake a long pilgrimage to a famous hermitage in order that God might grant her request. This pilgrimage lasted thirteen days. Catalina dressed herself in sackcloth and walked barefoot to the hermitage situated at the top of a high mountain.[3] At the top of this mountain there was a picture of St Bridget, which had been venerated for years, because of the many miracles that had been granted there.[4] Within two weeks, Catalina's prayers had been answered and John of Avila had been conceived. He would be a bright light that would touch the hearts of many, in his time and in our own.[5]

From a very early age, John had a great love for God and displayed such virtue that those around him were often astounded. From the age of five, John was often found in the middle of the night, deep in prayer and contemplation. There were also times when John did not return home from school and when someone was sent to look for him, he would be found in a church, in deep conversion with the Lord in the Blessed Sacrament.[6] John felt a strong attraction to the priesthood from when he was very young; therefore, whenever he went to church, he would return home and imitate the celebration of the Mass at his own little altar.[7]

Both of John's parents were converts to the Catholic Faith. John's father was from 'Jewish ancestry, and his mother may also have been Jewish,'[8] this often made things difficult for the family.[9] During this period in Spain, there were what they called 'new Christians' — those who had converted to the Catholic Faith — and 'old Christians' — those who had been born to Catholic parents. Many Jewish converts in Spain became devout and fervent Catholics and held high political and ecclesiastical positions. There were some however, who had been baptized but continued to practice the Jewish faith, and encouraged others to do so. At that time — the late fifteenth century — the Catholic monarchs Ferdinand and Isabella had reclaimed Granada from the hands of the Muslims.[10] One of the main tasks of the Spanish Inquisition was to ensure that Jewish converts were not working against the Christian Faith.[11] In 1492 the monarchs of Spain, with encouragement from some of the inquisitors, decided to take extreme measures to defend the faith. They ordered all Jews who had not converted to the Christian faith to leave Spain. In reaction to this, many Jews decided to be baptised, without having truly converted, so that they could remain in Spain. As a consequence, instead of things becoming better in Spain, they only became worse. Since these people had converted under duress, they had little knowledge of the faith, and often continued to practise Judaism and all of the Jewish customs. Unfortunately this meant that most Jewish converts, even those who had embraced the Christian faith, rarely found welcome among the old Christians and the Spanish people looked upon them with suspicion. John of Avila had firsthand experience of this unfortunate reality, because he was born within a decade of the expulsion of the Jews from Spain. He often experienced animosity because his parents were Jewish converts. This whole experience influenced John's years as a priest; he opposed all discrimination against people because of their lineage and he insisted upon the 'dignity of Jewish and Muslim converts', so much so that John wrote a whole section in his work *Audi Filia* about the importance of recognising that since we are all Christians, we should not have any vanity about our lineage.[12]

This whole experience did not deter John of Avila in any way. He loved God and loved his Catholic Faith. He was a very bright young boy, and by the age of fourteen he had completed a course in rhetoric and humanities. His intelligence and the abilities he displayed prompted John's father to send him to Salamanca University to study law.[13] He studied with great diligence; however his heart and his thoughts were on higher things. John felt more and more drawn to lead a life of perfection and to seek nothing but Christ. Nevertheless, he continued with his studies in law. Finally, he decided to inform his father of his ardent desire to live more deeply for Christ and his disinclination to continue with his studies. His father was very understanding and allowed John to leave Salamanca and return home. Upon John's return, he begged his parents to give him the use of a very small room in their house. There, John occupied himself with prayer and a life of solitude.[14]

Life as a Hermit and the Path to Priesthood

John lived in this room for almost three years; he lived the life of a hermit, and left the house only in the case of necessity or for devotion. He ate very little food and slept on a plank or sometimes on some brushwood which had been put in a corner. It was difficult for Alfonso and Catalina to see their son deprive himself so much and undertake such hard penances. However, they did not complain for fear that they would interfere with God's plan.[15] John was left in peace to continue his life as a hermit in his family's house. One day a Franciscan religious, who was a holy man, came to visit the town of Almodóvar where John lived. When the holy religious heard people in this district speak of John's piety and holiness, he decided to try and meet with John. He visited John at his parent's house and was amazed to find a young man with so much spiritual maturity and perfection. He spoke immediately with John's parents and advised them that John should study philosophy and theology, because in this way, he would be able to better serve the Church. When John heard this advice, he strongly believed that it was the will of God and with the consent of his parents, he began his studies in philosophy and theology.[16] He went to the University of Alcalá and studied under Dominic del Soto, who was well known for his commentaries on St Thomas Aquinas.[17]

Before John had completed his studies in philosophy, both of his parents died. This was a great loss to him, and he turned to God even more than he had done previously. At the University, John soon acquired a reputation as a man of great holiness and intelligence. He completed all of his studies in theology and philosophy and became a model for all those at the University who came after him.[18] When John's parents died they left him their estate. John, however, desiring to live a life of strict poverty, sold the estate and gave the proceeds to the poor.[19] In 1526 John was finally ordained to the priesthood.[20] His first Mass was offered for his parents in Almodóvar del Campo, at the church where his parents had been buried. He prepared for this holy occasion by rigorous fasts, vigils, and holy acts of virtue.[21] It was an ancient custom in this part of Spain for a priest who was newly ordained to have a banquet for friends and relatives. Instead of inviting friends, Fr Avila decided to invite twelve very poor people to his house; he gave them a sumptuous meal, bathed their feet and gave them new clothes to wear.[22]

Fr Avila had great desires when he became a priest to go to the Americas. Less than ten years before John was born, Christopher Columbus had discovered the 'New World'. This opened up a great mission field on the other side of the ocean. At the same time, there was still much need for renewing the Catholic Faith in Spain.[23] John had lived in Spain his whole life and wanted to go to the Americas as a missionary and die a martyr's death, but God had different plans. Fr Ferdinand Contreras, a devout priest, recognised John's exceptional holiness and set out to dissuade our Saint from undertaking his missionary journey to the Americas. He informed Fr Avila of Spain's great need for sanctification and how much he would be able to help in this great mission if he remained in Spain. John, ever faithful and obedient to his Bishop, to whom he had already promised he would travel to the Americas as a missionary, could not be swayed.[24] Fr Contreras was not discouraged. He went immediately to see the Archbishop of Seville, who was the Inquisitor General and informed him about the great treasure in their diocese. On hearing this news the Archbishop, not wanting to lose such a holy man, went to try to pursued Fr Avila to remain in Spain. Determined to keep his promise to his Bishop, John declined. The Archbishop kindly and with great firmness left Fr Avila no choice and ordered him to remain in Spain out of obedience. No sooner had the Archbishop said this when Fr Avila replied, 'My lord, since this is the Divine will for me, may it be fulfilled. I am content.'[25] John began his priestly ministry in Seville, and great numbers of people flocked to the church to hear him preach.[26] His missionary work had begun, the work which would earn John the title 'Apostle of Andalusia'.[27] Fr Avila remained in Serville and devoted himself to his priestly ministry. He also continued with his studies in theology at the College of St Thomas, where he was given the title of 'Master.'[28]

Helping the Poor

Throughout Fr Avila's ministry, he assisted people with their spiritual needs and helped the poor who were in need of food and clothing. In addition to his own inheritance which he had distributed to the poor, John was constantly receiving money from wealthy people. These wealthy people had so much confidence in John of Avila that they asked him to distribute their charitable funds where he saw fit, for they trusted that each penny would be used where it was most needed and for the glory of God.[29] There was no work that was too difficult or expensive for Fr Avila if he believed that it was for God's greater glory. To those who tried to tell Fr Avila that he did not have enough money to provide for a certain need, he would reply, 'But God, does He count for nothing? If a rich merchant were to give me letters to all his agents, in order that I might have money at my command, I would consider myself well provided, and safe; should I not, therefore, trust in God, a Lord so much richer, a Friend so much more faithful and infallible in His promises?'. When others needed help, he was always able to provide for them abundantly. He would say, 'What both confounds and encourages me is, that I never give anything to God without His speedily repaying me a hundredfold.'[30]

John of Avila always lived very simply and when he was invited to preach in various towns he would never accept the invitations from lords, who invited him to stay in their beautiful palaces, but preferred to reside with his fellow priests in very basic accommodations.[31] John remained forever detached from material goods. Nearly everything he received he gave away, so much so that in later years, St Teresa of Avila wrote in a letter to her brother Lorenzo concerning Fr Avila, 'When you wish to do him a kindness, do it by way of alms, for he is very poor, and exceedingly disengaged from riches.'[32] Fr Avila was constantly at the service of others; after spending many hours in prayer and celebrating the Holy Sacrifice of the Mass, he would spend his remaining hours serving the poor, visiting those in the hospital and in prison. He brought great consolation to many souls.[33]

Preaching

Preaching was one of Fr Avila's greatest gifts. When he was preparing to preach, he would spend a couple of hours before the crucifix, and sometimes he would even spend the whole night in prayer, begging God to convert souls that were coming to hear him.[34] In prayer, he would gain great wisdom as to how he should treat the subject matter for his sermons.[35] He would also advise his listeners to prepare well before coming to hear him preach: 'We need the Holy Ghost to infuse Himself into our hearts, to soften them and set them alight with the gift of His divine fire.'[36] The aim of Fr Avila's preaching was always to draw people to the heart God. If people were not already living a holy life, he would urge them to turn away from their sins and come to receive forgiveness from a loving and merciful God. If people were already living a moral life then he would encourage them to draw even closer to the heart of God.

When the Apostle of Andalusia preached his first homily on the Feast of St Mary Magdalene, in the Cathedral of Seville, he was not at all confident. When he saw the crowds of people standing before him he was unable to speak; he was filled with doubts and confusion. After some time however, he fixed his eyes on a crucifix and began to pray. Immediately he felt changed and his preaching proved to be so powerful that his listeners were filled with awe at the power of his speech. This was the beginning of our Saint's life as a great preacher and director of consciences.[37] He became so well known for his moving sermons that there was often an overflow of people outside of the church; during his sermons the sound of weeping was heard regularly.[38] Our Saint often preached about the great importance of personal renewal, especially in his sermons about the Holy Spirit.[39] A holy Dominican priest and brilliant theologian Fr Augustine Saluzio said that 'for several centuries no orator had been heard in Spain so truly apostolic as Fr Avila, and that he had been sent by God for the reformation of morals, and for the sanctification of all that country'.[40]

Fr Avila taught that the 'secret of preaching' is much study and even more prayer, especially before the crucifix.[41] A young priest once asked him how he too could acquire such a powerful skill of preaching. The holy preacher replied, 'There is no other way, but ardent love of God.'[42] There are so many instances where the effect of John of Avila's preaching touched and converted souls. Fr Avila tried to touch all the people who came to listen to his sermons. Whenever he was invited to preach, he always emphasised the use of the catechism, which at the time was being greatly neglected. He would often be seen teaching catechism to crowds of small children; he taught them with precision but with great simplicity adapting to their capabilities.[43]

Two of the most famous conversions attributed to the preaching of Fr Avila are those of St Francis Borgia and St John of God.[44] Upon hearing one of his sermons, the Portuguese man, who would later become known as St John of God, was filled with horror and contrition at the thought of his sins and is said to have run out of the church crying 'Mercy, Mercy'.[45] After deciding to dedicate his life to God, St John of God continued to receive guidance from Fr Avila until his death.[46] Francis Borgia, also received advice from Fr Avila after listening to his sermon. Fr Avila instructed him on how to live a perfect life in the service of God and prophesied that one day Francis would do great work for the glory of God.[47]

Confession and Spiritual Direction

News of John's holiness had spread throughout the whole of Spain and he became known as a priest who was highly skilled in directing souls.[48] St Teresa of Avila in a letter to her brother wrote, 'You may speak to Juan de Avila about anything, for he is a very good man. You tell me he often talks to you: I am glad of it. Visit him sometimes … he is, in my opinion, one of the best priests you have at Avila.'[49] This holy Apostle of Andalusia was extremely compassionate in all his dealings with the faithful. People said that 'he had a separate heart for each of those he loved, so that each one believed himself to be best beloved'.[50] He received everyone with such kindness and generosity and never showed any sign of impatience or annoyance. Whenever Fr Avila tried to correct someone's faults he spoke firmly but with so much sweetness that instead of becoming offended, the person seemed to love him all the more.[51]

No matter what the trial or temptation, Fr Avila had a remarkable way of bringing comfort and relief. He treated everyone with so much compassion that he quickly earned their trust and encouraged them to bear with their trials. Venerable Luis of Granada, a very close friend and disciple of Fr Avila, wrote, 'It is difficult to say whether John won most souls to Christ by his teaching or by the greatness of his charity and love in his exercise of good works towards all. He loved them, and accommodated himself to their need, as if he were the Father of all, making himself, as the Apostle says, all things to all men, that he might save all.'[52] Thus he truly imitated St Paul, whom he had taken as his model and guide; he never ceased to follow his example.[53]

It was Master Avila's custom to invite his listeners, at the end of his sermon, to go to the sacrament of confession.[54] Our Saint encouraged everyone to throw themselves into the arms of God's loving Mercy and assured them that God would forgive even the most heinous crimes if they were truly ready to amend their ways.[55] Even when John was extremely tired after preaching, he did not turn away the penitents who came to him for confession. He often remained in the confessional for up to four or five hours.[56] Whenever someone asked Fr Avila to take more care of himself, he replied, 'How can I do that, when I belong not to myself, but to others?'.[57]

The Inquisition

Those who work tirelessly for God's glory and the salvation of souls often meet with opposition; such was the case for Fr Avila. There were a number of wealthy people who were offended after hearing one of his sermons. They reported Fr Avila to the Inquisition; they alleged that he had taught that the rich could not enter the kingdom of heaven. Consequently Fr Avila was kept in custody until the whole matter could be examined.[58] Fr Avila was accused before the Inquisition and detained in prison for one year.[59] He remained in discomfort and solitude. Nevertheless, he displayed great patience, gentleness and kindness through the whole ordeal and humbly submitted to whatever happened.[60] This whole experience served to bring Fr Avila into closer union with God. He said that 'the Divine light which flooded his soul in the darkness of prison was so vivid, enabling him to recognize more and more the greatness of God, and the immense riches which we have in Jesus Christ.'[61] Luis of Granada visited Fr Avila in prison; there our Saint revealed to him that during his time in the prison, he had been filled with consolations and had received 'new light on the mysteries of Redemption'.[62] Fr Avila was finally acquitted and was incardinated into the Diocese of Córdoba, where he continued to touch hearts through his preaching and ministry.[63]

Guiding Priestly Formation

Master Avila had a profound awareness of the dignity of the priesthood, and this led him to seek the road of perfection with great diligence. Many priests and those preparing for priesthood tried to follow Fr Avila's example; he had become a true model for priests in Spain during his lifetime.[64] He always encouraged all the priests he met, corresponding with them and constantly reminding them of the great importance of preparing well for the Holy Sacrifice of the Mass. He also reminded them of the high dignity of the priest-hood and their obligation to lead a life that would witness to such a holy state.[65] One of John's chief concerns was the sanctification of the clergy. He understood the importance of the need of their Christian witness and example to those around them.[66] Since Fr Avila was so concerned with both the intellectual and moral condition of the clergy, he endeavoured to raise the standards of both. He was shocked and grieved to see the indifference with which men put themselves forward for ordination to the priesthood. He remarked that these men seemed 'altogether to lose sight of the solemn duties and responsibilities of the ecclesiastical life, and merely to look to the possible emoluments and advantages which it opened up to them'.[67]

Whilst Fr Avila lived in Seville, priests and men desiring to become priests began to gather around him. These men became Fr Avila's disciples, and they joined together in a semi structured fraternal life together.[68] Master Avila also founded various schools of learning; there were numerous schools which opened in Spain which acknowledged Fr Avila as their founder. He worked with great ardour to multiply colleges for the instruction of those who felt called to the priesthood; he did this with the help of bishops and benefactors, and all of these colleges were under his advice and direction.[69] Several of these 'minor and major colleges … after the Council of Trent would become seminaries along the lines laid down by that Council.'[70]

One of Master Avila's biggest undertakings was the University of Baeza. He became involved with the founding of this university because of a wealthy and devout man by the name of Doctor Rodriguez Lopez, who lived in Baeza. This man was interested in founding a university for the study of science and a college for young men who felt called to priesthood. Having heard of the virtuous Apostle of Andalusia, Lopez wanted no other than this holy Saint to help him; so he took his ideas to the Pope who approved his plans. Fr Avila accepted the position in humble obedience and was made superior of the university,[71] which soon became known throughout Spain and became a model to imitate.[72] It was also 'known for centuries for its work of training clerics and laity'.[73]

Such was Fr Avila's understanding of the impor- tance of learning that whenever he met youth who had more than an average capacity for it and were unable to pay for an education, he would take it upon himself to provide all the necessary funding.[74] As much as Fr Avila believed in the importance of education, he never lost sight of the even greater importance of prayer. When one of Fr Avila's spiritual disciples gave him an account of his daily activities, he replied, 'Brother, a little less study, and a little more prayer; in this way you will learn much within a brief space, [and] God becomes better known.'[75]

The Society of Jesus

St Ignatius of Loyola founded the Society of Jesus in Fr Avila's lifetime. When our Saint learned that one of the chief aims of the Society was to found schools for instruction in 'letters and piety,' he rejoiced.[76] When John saw the exemplary way of life of this new order, their detachment from worldly things and their great zeal and labours for the salvation of souls, his love for them grew even more.[77] Fr Avila had such a love for the Society that he spread word of the school continually and encouraged a great number of his disciples to enter the order,[78] one of whom was St Francis Borgia, who became one of St Ignatius's first disciples. Fr Avila's admiration and affection for the Society remained with him, and he was always there to encourage them and help them through the difficulties they experienced in their first beginnings in Spain.[79]

Before Fr Avila had heard of the Society, he had made plans to start something very similar. The great Doctor of the Church St Francis de Sales, in his work *Treatise on the Love of God*, wrote of Fr Avila's desire and extolled his docility to the will of God:

John of Avila, that holy and learned preacher of Andalusia, having a design to form a company of reformed priests for the advancement of God's glory, and having already made good progress in the matter, as soon as he saw the Jesuits in the field, thinking they were enough for that time, immediately stopped his own undertaking, with an incomparable meekness and humility. Oh how blessed are such souls, bold and strong in the undertakings God proposes to them, and withal tractable and facile in giving them over when God so disposes! These are marks of a most perfect indifference, to leave off doing a good when God pleases, and to return from half way when God's will, which is our guide, ordains it.[80]

The Passion of Christ and the Blessed Sacrament

Master Avila's spiritual life was centred around Christ's passion.[81] It was his custom to keep sacred Thursday night and Friday of every week in remembrance of Christ's agony in the garden and His passion on the Cross.[82] Of course, Fr Avila, like all the Saints, had a great love for our Lord in the Blessed Sacrament and understood the great strength we can draw from this most precious gift. He wrote of the 'true fire which may kindle and enflame us, and this is *Jesus Christ* our Lord, in the *Blessed Sacrament*'.[83] Fr Avila recommended that there was no better way to receive our Lord in the Blessed Sacrament than with 'consideration, and love of his *passion*,' and a 'lively and strong Faith'.[84] Our Saint never missed an opportunity to promote frequent reception of Holy Communion. Although there were others who disagreed with him, he never desisted, saying that 'the Church possessed no other means more opportune and efficacious than these for the reform of morals.' He always emphasized, however, the dispositions which are necessary for receiving Holy Communion,[85] especially after an encounter he had with Jesus on the Feast of Corpus Domini. The Lord made known to him just how badly Christians were treating Him. Our Saint was left grieving at the thought of such terrible abuse and henceforth, when this Feast was approaching he would go to great lengths to see that this Feast was celebrated with reverence and devotion.[86]

The Holy Spirit and the Blessed Virgin

Master Avila had deep devotion to the Holy Spirit, and constantly preached about the great need we have for Him in our lives. He exhorted all people, priests, religious and lay, to be ready to follow the impulses of the Holy Spirit in order to reach Christian perfection, to which everyone is called.[87] The Feast of Pentecost was most dear to Fr of Avila; he would spend the week before this beautiful feast in prayer and fasting, preparing to receive the outpouring of His gifts. Fr Avila also encouraged others to prepare for this wonderful Feast. When our Saint preached about the Holy Spirit, he would exclaim with great joy, 'Oh, if I could but kindle within you some devotion to this truly consoling Spirit! I feel certain that in a few hours you would become completely changed; open your heart to Him, and allow Him to imprint His Divine teaching upon you, and you will see.'[88] Fr Avila invited all his listeners to pray to the Holy Spirit so that they could be transformed and experience true peace.[89] Master Avila said that the Blessed Mother, who had an intense love for the Holy Spirit, would help us in our relationship with Him: 'She is deeply loved by the Holy Ghost and He by her. He knows her purity of heart ... Let us beseech her who is so loved by the Holy Ghost to obtain for us the grace to speak of this important guest.'[90]

Fr Avila had a profound love for the Blessed Mother; he always put himself in the hands of Mary and trusted in her loving protection and intercession. Our Saint also taught his listeners to give her the honour that she truly deserves, promoting especially her Immaculate Conception, which he often spoke about to the youth in order to promote a love for purity.[91] Our Saint exhorted everyone to pray to the Blessed Virgin in order that she would 'obtain for us her adopted children the grace to help us do right, never to speak evil, and the grace of a happy death.'[92]

The Final Years

Our Saint spent the final years of his life in Montilla Andalusia, in the Diocese of Córdoba. Even though he went through tremendous bodily suffering, whenever he could he continued to hear confessions, preach, give spiritual direction and conferences to priests and Jesuit novices. He also continued to write letters to people in different states of life.[93] He worked as long as he could until finally worn out from his labours, he was close to passing from this world. The rector of Fr Avila's college said to him, 'What joy it must be to you to think of meeting the Saviour!'. However, John replied 'Ah! Rather do I tremble... at the thought of my sins.'[94] When it was time for this holy Saint to go and meet God, he received the last Sacrament, and kissing the crucifix which he held in his hands, calmly and peacefully departed into everlasting life.[95] Fr Avila died on May 10, 1569. He had requested burial in the Jesuit church in the town Montilla, and his request was granted.[96] When St Teresa of Avila heard the news that Fr Avila had gone to his heavenly home she was said to have wept bitterly. When asked why she was weeping—for St John of Avila was surely in heaven— she replied, 'This I do not doubt, but what troubles me is, that the Church of God has lost a strong pillar, and many souls a powerful support; though living at a distance, I myself was under great obligation to him.'[97]

Canonisation and Works

John of Avila was beatified by Pope Leo XIII on 6 April 1894, and in 1946 Pope Pius XII acknowledged him as an outstanding model for priests and named him Patron of the diocesan clergy of Spain.[98] He was then canonized on 31 May 1970 by Pope Paul VI.[99] Finally on 7 October 2012 Pope Benedict XVI declared St John of Avila a Doctor of the Church. St John of Avila has left us with a number of works which are packed with insight and wisdom. Through the centuries his 'writings have been a source of inspiration for priestly spirituality'.[100] They are also a rich treasure for all those who desire to follow the Gospel message and need help with discernment along the way. St Francis de Sales, Doctor of the Church, in his well known work *Introduction to the Devout Life* advises us to read the works of St John of Avila with great care: 'Read some small portion attentively, as though you were reading letters sent by the Saints from Paradise to teach you the way thither, and encourage you to follow them.'[101]

Master Avila's major work, *Audi Filia*, is a classic of spirituality and his most systematic work. He worked on this book at different periods of his life; the final edition was finished during the last few years of his life.[102] *Audi Filia* is one of the most important spiritual treasures of the rich period of the sixteenth century.[103] Fr Avila began writing *Audi Filia* at the request of Dona Sancha Carrillo, a young lady who needed something that could serve as advice for living out her spiritual life.[104] This young Spanish woman converted after having been persuaded by her brother to go to the Sacrament of Confession with Fr Avila. Until meeting with the Saint, this young woman was living a very worldly life. However, after her confession, she was completely changed. She turned her life around and decided to take Christ as her Spouse thus making a lifetime vow of virginity at the advice of Fr Avila.[105] Fr Avila began writing *Audi Filia* when he was imprisoned between 1532 and 1533. The work is structured around Ps 45:11–12, consists of six parts, and has a total of 113 chapters. The edition that we have today has been expanded and revised; it is a version which he wrote for all Christians who want to follow Christ and reach perfection. Master Avila says that the 'purpose of the book is to give some Christian instructions and rules for beginners in God's service so that, through his grace, they may know how to put their desires into effect'.[106]

Master Avila wrote many letters to his directees during his years as a priest, giving spiritual advice; they have always been 'regarded as models of spiritual guidance'.[107] Commenting on Fr Avila's *Letters*, Luis of Granada writes: 'Every competent judge who reads these letters, and takes into account the variety of the matter, the dignity of the language, the force of reasoning, the amount of Scripture treated of in it, and above all, the ease and readiness of its composition, at once recognizes the presence of the finger of God.'[108] There are also many good theologians who have declared that from Fr Avila's *Letters* alone 'in their opinion, he would deserve to be called a "Doctor of the Church"'.[109] We also have many of Fr Avila's sermons in written form. His disciples often took notes whilst Fr Avila preached, and then, when he had time, Fr Avila would help with any corrections that were needed. These sermons are rich in the use of Sacred Scripture and give witness to how he engaged all of his listeners through lively dialogue form by posing questions and then giving answers.[110]

During his lifetime Fr Avila also wrote a 'pedagogical synthesis of the content of the faith, addressed to children and adults'.[111] This was often used by Fr Avila and 'Saint Thomas of Villanova, Archbishop of Valencia, … disseminated Fr Avila's catechetical method in his diocese and throughout the south of Spain.'[112] Master Avila also wrote a *Treatise on the Priesthood* which is a brief compendium including his conversations, sermons and letters.[113] This work was written in preparation for various conferences Fr Avila was going to give concerning renewal of the priesthood.[114] In addition, Master Avila wrote the *Memoriales*, which had quite a lot of influence on the assembly at the Council of Trent. They dealt with ecclesial and personal renewal. The Archbishop of Granada was hoping to take Fr Avila with him to the second and third periods of the Council. However, because of his ill health, Master Avila was unable to accompany him and therefore drafted the *Memoriales*.[115] Fr Avila also wrote various Scripture commentaries which Pope Benedict XVI says are 'systematic expositions of remarkable insight and of great pastoral value'.[116] He also refers to Fr Avila's work the *Treatise on the Love of God* as a 'literary gem,' and a 'pearl of Spanish literature on ascetical theology' which 'reflects the depths of his insight into the mystery of Christ, the Incarnate Word and Redeemer'.[117]

Notes

1   Pope Benedict XVI, *Apostolic Letter Proclaiming Saint John of Avila, diocesan priest, a Doctor of the Universal Church* (Vatican City: Libreria Editrice Vaticana, 2012), 2. (Hereafter cited as *Apostolic Letter*.)

2   Longaro degli Oddi, *Life of the Blessed Master John of Avila; Secular Priest, Called the Apostle of Andulusia* (London: Burns and Oates, 1898), p. 4.

3   *Ibid.*

4   *Ibid.*, pp. 4–5.

5   *Ibid.*, p. 5.

6   *Ibid.*

7   *Ibid.*, p. 8.

8   John of Avila, *Audi, Filia—Listen, O Daughter*, translated and introduced by Joan Frances Gormley (New York: Paulist Press, 2006), p. 5. (Hereafter cited as *AF*.)

9   *AF*, Intro. p. 5.

10 *Ibid.*, p. 1.

11 *Ibid.*, pp. 5–6.

12 *Ibid.*

13 Oddi, *Life of the Blessed Master John of Avila*, p. 6.

14 *Ibid.*

15 *Ibid.*

16 *Ibid.*, pp. 6–7.

17 Marguerite Tollemanche, *Spanish Mystics: A Sequel to Many Voices* (Whitefish, MT: Kessinger Publishing, 2005), p. 13.

18 Oddi, *Life of the Blessed Master John of Avila*, p. 8.

19 *AF*, Intro. p. 5.

20   John of Avila, *Letters of Blessed John of Avila*, translated and selected from the Spanish by the Benedictines of Stanbrook (London: Burns & Oates Ltd, 1904), Preface, p. 10. (Hereafter cited as *Letters.*)

21   Oddi, *Life of the Blessed Master John of Avila*, pp. 8–9.

22   *Ibid.*, p. 9.

23   *AF,* Intro. p. 1.

24   Oddi, *Life of the Blessed Master John of Avila*, pp. 9–10.

25   *Ibid.*, pp. 10–11.

26   *Ibid.*, p. 11.

27   *AF,* Intro. p. 10.

28   *Apostolic Letter*, 2.

29   Oddi, *Life of the Blessed Master John of Avila*, p. 63.

30   *Ibid.*, p. 60.

31   *Ibid.*, p. 79.

32   Teresa of Avila, *The Letters of St Teresa*, translated by Rev. John Dalton (London: Thomas Baker, 1902), No. XXXII. To Lorenzo de Cepeda, Brother of the Saint.

33   Oddi, *Life of the Blessed Master John of Avila*, p. 15.

34   *Ibid.*, p. 13.

35   *Ibid.*, p. 65.

36   John of Avila, *The Holy Ghost,* translated by Ena Dargan (Dublin: Scepter Limited, 1959), IV, p. 81. (Hereafter cited as *HG.*)

37   Tollemanche, *Spanish Mystics*, p. 14.

38   Oddi, *Life of the Blessed Master John of Avila*, p. 15.

39   Rady Roldan-Figueroa, 'Espirituación: Juan de Ávila's Doctrine of Union with the Holy Spirit' in *Renaissance and Reformation / Renaissance et Réforme* vol. XXIX / issue 2–3 (2005), 81.

40   Oddi, *Life of the Blessed Master John of Avila*, p. 12.

41   *AF,* Intro. p. 14.

42   Tollemache, *Spanish Mystics*, p. 14.

43   Oddi, *Life of the Blessed Master John of Avila*, p. 38.

44   *Letters*, Preface, p. 6.

45   Oddi, *Life of the Blessed Master John of Avila*, p. 26.

46   *Ibid.*, p. 29.

47   *Ibid.,* pp. 25–26.

48   *Ibid.,* p. 46.

49   *The Letters of St Teresa,* No. XXXII. To Lorenzo de Cepeda, Brother of the Saint.

50   Tollemanche, *Spanish Mystics,* p. 15.

51   Oddi, *Life of the Blessed Master John of Avila,* pp. 61–62.

52   *Ibid.,* p. 98.

53   *Ibid.,* p. 61.

54   *Ibid.,* p. 15.

55   *Ibid.,* p. 61.

56   *Ibid.,* p. 46.

57   *Ibid.,* p. 61.

58   *Ibid.,* p. 16.

59   Roldan-Figueroa, 'Juan de Ávila's Doctrine of Union with the Holy Spirit', p. 73.

60   *AF,* Intro. p. 16.

61   Oddi, *Life of the Blessed Master John of Avila,* p. 17.

62   Tollemanche, *Spanish Mystics,* p. 16.

63   *Apostolic Letter,* 2.

64   Oddi, *Life of the Blessed Master John of Avila,* p. 9.

65   *Ibid.,* p. 74.

66   *Ibid.,* pp. 15–16.

67   Tollemanche, *Spanish Mystics,* p. 19.

68   *AF,* Intro. pp. 10–11.

69   Oddi, *Life of the Blessed Master John of Avila,* p. 38.

70   *Apostolic Letter,* 2.

71   Oddi, *Life of the Blessed Master John of Avila,* p. 37.

72   *Ibid.,* p. 38.

73   *Apostolic Letter,* 2.

74   Oddi, *Life of the Blessed Master John of Avila,* p. 39.

75   *Ibid.,* p. 66.

76   *Ibid.,* p. 39.

77   *Ibid.,* p. 56.

78   *Ibid.,* p. 39.

79   *Letters,* Preface, 7.

80   Francis de Sales, *Treatise on the Love of God*, translated by Henry Benedict Mackey (Rockford, IL: Tan Books and Publishers, Inc., 1997), ch. VI, 316–317.

81   *AF,* Intro. p. 9.

82   Tollemanche, *Spanish Mystics*, p. 15.

83   John of Avila, *Certain Selected Spiritual Epistles* (Rouen: John Le Costurier, 1631), 3, pp. 22–23. (Hereafter cited as *Epistles.*)

84   *Epistles,* 3, p. 23.

85   Oddi, *Life of the Blessed Master John of Avila,* p. 72.

86   *Ibid.*, p. 71.

87   *HG,* Intro. p. 8.

88   *Ibid.*, p. 68.

89   Roldan-Figueroa, 'Juan de Ávila's Doctrine of Union with the Holy Spirit', p. 72.

90   *HG,* IV, pp. 82–83.

91   Oddi, *Life of the Blessed Master John of Avila,* p. 68.

92   *HG,* II, p. 30.

93   *AF,* Intro. p. 16.

94   Tollemanche, *Spanish Mystics*, p. 21.

95   *Ibid.*

96   *AF,* Intro. p. 16.

97   Oddi, *Life of the Blessed Master John of Avila,* p. 84.

98   *Apostolic Letter,* 7.

99   Anna Hamling, 'John of Avila' in *The Encyclopedia of Christian Literature,* edited by George Thomas Kurian & James D. Smith, III, vol. 1, Genres and Types/Biographies A–G (Lanham, MD: Scarecrow Press, Inc. 2010), p. 392.

100   *Apostolic Letter,* 6.

101   Francis de Sales, *Introduction to the Devout Life* (Rockford, IL: Tan Books and Publishers, Inc., 2010), Part II, ch. XVII.

102   *Apostolic Letter,* 4.

103   *AF,* Intro. p. 21.

104   *Ibid.*

105   Oddi, *Life of the Blessed Master John of Avila,* pp. 31–32.

106   *AF,* Intro. pp. 21–22.

107   Tollemanche, *Spanish Mystics*, p. 15.

[108] Oddi, *Life of the Blessed Master John of Avila,* p. 63.

[109] *Letters,* Preface, 11.

[110] *AF,* Intro. p. 17.

[111] *Apostolic Letter,* 4.

[112] *Ibid.,* 3.

[113] *Ibid.,* 4.

[114] *AF,* Intro. p. 20

[115] *Apostolic Letter,* 2, 4.

[116] *Ibid.,* 4.

[117] *Ibid.*

2

THE NEED FOR GRACE AND THE WHOLE SUPERNATURAL ORGANISM

THE WORKS OF St John of Avila are packed with wise advice concerning growth in the spiritual life and how one can advance toward union with God. Fr Avila was known by his contemporaries as a 'great doctor of mystical theology, and most experienced master in the direction of souls'.[1] His spiritual guidance and wisdom are also most useful today for helping those who desire to draw closer to Christ and advance on their spiritual journey. There are a number of main themes which run throughout Fr Avila's works. He emphasises the importance of faith and trusting in a loving and merciful God, the necessity of humility verses pride, the importance of grace, and responding to the inspiration of God's grace. Fr Avila also gives a wealth of information about spiritual discernment. It is evident that Fr Avila's whole spiritual vision is rooted in Christ Crucified; he highly recommends meditating on Christ's Passion as an aid to growth in holiness.

This chapter will look specifically at the need for God's grace, the theological virtues and the seven gifts of the Holy Spirit. These topics can be found throughout St John of Avila's works, but they are not all together in one place. Therefore, without already having a clear understanding of how the whole supernatural organism fits together, one might miss the theological gems which Fr Avila presents. This information highlights the beautiful reality of the life of grace that exists within a soul which is in a state of grace. It will also show the need to respond to God's inspirations and the importance of constantly striving for greater holiness. Fr Avila is truly an outstanding Saint and Doctor of the Church to whom we can look for advice in spiritual matters. St Ignatius of Loyola, a contemporary of Fr Avila, says that he is a 'man full of God, a great doctor of mystical theology, an excellent master of Christian perfection'.[2]

The State of Innocence

Before the Fall, our first parents, Adam and Eve, lived happily in friendship with God in the garden of Eden. They were in a state of grace,[3] which means they enjoyed sanctifying grace, which perfects the soul. As a consequence of this grace, all of their thoughts and actions were ordered toward God[4] – they knew God and were able to love Him above all things.[5] God had created Adam and Eve with a physical body animated by a spiritual soul. Their human nature was not wounded or damaged. In addition to their natural gifts, He also gave them a share in His own life by giving them certain supernatural gifts. He gave them the Holy Spirit. As our Saint would often say, 'God breathed into man bodily life and also spiritual life. He gave him the Holy Ghost.'[6] By grace, Adam and Eve were always able to obey God; their reason was completely subject to Him. This was not 'merely a natural gift, but a supernatural endowment of grace.'[7] Their flesh was also subjected to their will, and the passions followed perfectly whatever their will desired, without ever rebelling.[8] For this reason, they enjoyed perfect peace; they had peace within their own heart, peace between each other, and peace with God. Thus, they lived in the 'state of innocence, with their passions obeying reason and reason obeying God.'[9]

After the Fall

The grace of God, by which Adam and Eve were at peace and were so ordered, did not in any way impede their free will; they were still free to choose between good and evil. God had entrusted them with the entire garden, with the exception of the fruit of one tree. Unfortunately as we know, the serpent called God a liar,[10] and Adam and Eve believed him; they decided to eat the fruit which God had forbidden, thus breaching the trust and friendship they had shared with God in the garden. As a consequence, they forfeited the life of grace and their friendship with God. The original sin caused the loss of grace, and their intellect was dulled and their will was greatly weakened.[11] Their flesh became insubordinate to their will and rebellious against their reason.[12] What God had made beautiful and well-ordered was made ugly by sin.[13] The soul that is not in a state of grace is no longer beautiful, for the 'spiritual light of grace and knowledge enlivening the beauty of the soul as colors do to the body, is also lacking; for the sinful soul is walking in darkness and is "made blacker than coal."'[14]

As children of Adam and Eve, we are born in a state of original sin and without the life of grace within our souls. In this wounded state, without the help of God's grace, we pursue our 'own private good'[15] and we fall into sin. Yet God does not wish the soul to perish;[16] out of His abundant goodness God desires to save all which He had made good and destroy all evil which had been committed.[17] Therefore, in His great love for mankind God sent His Only Begotten Son so that everyone can have the opportunity to receive healing and be transformed; for God wants to rescue the human soul 'in whom He once dwelt.'[18]

Through Grace We Participate in the Divine Life

John of Avila says, 'One single soul is more precious than all bodies already created and to be created.'[19] The value of one soul is extremely precious; the body is corruptible but the soul lasts forever and is destined for eternal life. God wants to lead each soul to final beatitude and happiness. In order to reach this ulti-mate happiness which is our final goal, we need God's gift of grace. Without God's grace the attainment of heaven is impossible; everyone is in need of God's saving help. To reach heaven is something beyond the capacity of human nature and therefore it is impossible for a person to merit life eternal without supernatural assistance.[20] Only with God's grace is this made possi-ble, for 'the gift of grace surpasses every capability of created nature, since it is nothing short of a partaking of the Divine Nature, which exceeds every other nature.'[21] God gives us a wonderful gift when He gives us the gift of life; however He gives us an even greater gift when He bestows on us the supernatural life.[22]

Through the gift of grace God heals the soul and raises it above the condition of its nature, so that it may participate in His Divine Goodness.[23] Fr Avila describes this reality as Christ clothing us in beauty.[24] This does not mean that the life of grace is completely distinct and separate from our natural lives; it is not something which is superimposed onto our natural human nature. Rather, it penetrates and transforms it. Whatever is good in our nature, grace perfects and transforms, directing us toward the Beatific Vision. Thus, grace does not destroy nature, but perfects it, elevates it, and makes it complete.[25] In other words, the 'grace of the Holy Spirit touches us in our "substance," in our personal being, and acts even at the level of our natural inclinations.'[26]

Baptism—God's Ineffable Gift

The Sacrament of 'Baptism is the basis of the whole Christian life, the gateway to life in the Spirit'.[27] Through this Sacrament, our sins are forgiven and by grace, we are justified—we are restored to friendship with God. We are baptised into the mysteries of our Lord's death and resurrection and thus we are incorporated into Jesus Christ. We become members of His Mystical Body. In the moment of holy Baptism, sanctifying grace is infused into our soul making us adopted children of God and pleasing to Him. The Holy Spirit begins to dwell within our soul, making us temples of God and we are spiritually born again.[28] No one can merit this grace; it is a gift which God gives out of his abundant goodness.[29] In the moment of Baptism, along with sanctifying grace, God gives the soul the three theological virtues—faith, hope, and charity—the infused moral virtues, and the seven gifts of the Holy Spirit, all of which are necessary for salvation. This 'ineffable gift' of grace and all that is needed for eternal life is merited for us by our Lord Jesus Christ.[30] The graced soul with all the infused virtues and gifts is referred to as the 'supernatural organism'. As the *Catechism of the Catholic Church* states:

The Most Holy Trinity gives the baptized sanctifying grace, the grace of *justification*: enabling
them to believe in God, to hope in him, and to
love him through the theological virtues; giving
them the power to live and act under the
prompting of the Holy Spirit through the gifts
of the Holy Spirit; allowing them to grow in
goodness through the moral virtues. Thus the
whole organism of the Christian's supernatural
life has its roots in Baptism.[31]

The Theological Virtue of Faith

'Faith is the realization of what is hoped for and
evidence of things not seen.'[32] Through faith we give
a simple assent to the truth and believe and adhere to
all that has been revealed through Christ and His
Church. Faith believes what it cannot see and gives
firm assent to that which remains hidden, because of
confidence in the One who reveals. This assent cannot
be given by the strength of our reason, for reason alone
cannot attain to the mysteries of faith.[33] God is 'so
bright that, as Saint Paul says, he dwells in a light that
no one can reach.'[34] Fr Avila explains, 'It is not that the
light is dark, but that it is a light that in every way
exceeds all understanding. It is the same as when we
see a wheel moving at the highest speed. We usually
say that the wheel is not stirring.'[35] Only God can give
us the strength to believe and He does this by infusing
faith into the intellect so that we are 'instructed and
fortified for this belief.'[36] Through grace the light of
faith transforms, heals, and perfects our understanding
and enlightens our intellect. Master Avila says that
faith 'inclines the understanding to believe the
supreme truth in what the Catholic Faith teaches… As
the needle of the compass is attracted by the force of

the North to be pointed toward it, so, by the faith that he infuses, God moves the understanding so that it goes toward him with an assent that is firm, tranquil, and full of satisfaction.'[37] Through faith God raises us above ourselves, and gives us 'supernatural strength with which to believe'.[38] This does not mean that to believe 'these things is contrary to reason or without reason.'[39] Rather, faith opens our eyes to see the light of truth; faith reveals a world of wonders and uncovers things that are concealed to the sole use of reason. In this way, through faith, to the Magi, was revealed 'the Incarnate God concealed beneath the appearance of a new-born Babe, and they adored Him, prostrate on the ground, confessing their own nothingness in His presence.'[40]

When we have true faith we believe with security and certainty, without scruple or doubt, regarding the things of God.[41] Faith gives us a certainty that exceeds all other types of certainties; through faith we know that we cannot be deceived.[42] Furthermore, Fr Avila explains that when 'this faith is perfect, it carries with it a light by which, though it does not see what it believes, it does see how worthy of belief are the things of God. Not only does it not experience difficulty in believing, but it experiences a very great delight, such as perfect virtue usually produces as it works with ease, strength, and delight.'[43]

In the moment of Baptism, we are justified by grace and faith, but not by faith alone. Fr Avila, who was a contemporary of Martin Luther, emphasised that justification is never given through faith alone; he would say that the doctrine of *sola fide* is a 'human invention.'[44] Master Avila explained that the Lord told St Mary Magdalene, 'Your faith has saved you, go in peace' (Lk 7:50); however, he also said 'her many sins are forgiven her because she has loved much' (Lk 7:47). Notice the Lord says both faith and love, for a person must have both; faith and love together are 'the cause and disposition for pardon'.[45] Indeed, St Paul never taught the doctrine of salvation by faith alone; instead, with great love for God, he admonished his hearers to 'work out your salvation with fear and trembling.'[46] God gives us faith, so that we can believe and follow all that He asks and so that this faith will be a 'light for the knowledge that helps move our will to love God and keep his commandments'.[47]

The Theological Virtue of Hope

'Man's great, true hope which holds firm in spite of all disappointments can only be God — God who has loved us and who continues to love us to the end, until all is accomplished.'[48] The theological virtue of hope, infused by God into the will, is that virtue 'by which we trust with complete certitude in the attainment of eternal life and the means necessary for reaching it' assisted by God's grace.[49] Fr Avila often spoke of this theological virtue in connection with the courage required to persevere in spiritual trials: 'We must be strengthened, not by confidence placed in ourselves, but by the firm hope we place in our Lord. This is what makes us victorious…'[50] Hope keeps us from discouragement, sustains us in times of abandonment, and opens our hearts in expectation of eternal beatitude.[51] As the *Catechism of the Catholic Church* states, 'Hope is the theological virtue by which we desire the kingdom of heaven and eternal life as our happiness, placing our trust in Christ's promises and relying not on our own strength, but on the help of the grace of the Holy Spirit.'[52]

The Theological Virtue of Charity and Friendship with God

'Faith, which sees the love of God revealed in the pierced heart of Jesus on the Cross, gives rise to love;'[53] God 'is love, and he who abides in love abides in God, and God abides in him'.[54] Charity is that theological virtue by which 'we love God above all things for his own sake, and our neighbor as ourselves for the love of God'.[55] Through God's gift of grace a person becomes a friend of God and is united to God through the theological virtue of charity.[56] Out of His abundant love for us God is always inviting us to friendship with Him; He waits patiently for us to open our hearts to Him. Fr Avila makes a beautiful analogy:

> The corporal sun diffuses itself liberally and goes about inviting whoever might want to receive it and gives its light to all who put no impediment. And if they do put an impediment, it is as if the sun insists that they remove it. If some hole or crack is found, however small, light enters through it and fills the house with light. If all this is so, what are we to say of the supreme divine Goodness that with such yearning and strength of love goes about surrounding its creatures, in order to give itself to them and fill them with color, with life, and with divine splendors?[57]

Our Christian life is one of grace and one of friendship with the three Divine Persons, with whom we are forever united as long as we remain in the state of grace. God is the only One Who can fulfil the desires of the human heart; He is the only one who can love us as we desire. The human person desires to love and to be loved. God made us so that we might 'love God, and loving Him posses Him, and possessing Him, enjoy Him, and enjoying Him, become blessed…and enter into a state of bliss.'[58] Therefore, God makes this friendship possible by giving us a share in His Divine Life, by giving us the life of grace within our soul. Thus, through God's grace we are raised to supernatural life and friendship with Him. We then have the capacity to love God with the love of charity. Since our own natural love would be inadequate, God gives us grace and charity with which we can truly love Him and have an intimate friendship with Him.[59] When God invites us to friendship with Him we should strive to live a holy life and follow the will of God; for Jesus says, 'You are My friends if you do the things that I command you' and 'If anyone love Me, he will keep my word'.[60] God does not leave us on our own however, to live out these commandments He gives us many gifts and graces so that we can live out this friendship with Him and grow in holiness and finally reach our end, eternal beatitude.

Meritorious Acts

Following the teaching of St Augustine, in his commentary to Psalm 102, the *Roman Missal* instructs us to pray, 'You are glorified in the assembly of your Holy Ones, for in crowning their merits you are crowning your own gifts.'[61] Merit is an effect of God's grace acting in us, and our cooperation with it.[62] 'Merit signifies the value of an act which makes it worthy of a reward.'[63] The Catholic understanding of supernatural merit 'arises from the fact that God has freely chosen to associate man with the work of his grace.'[64] St Paul instructs us, 'Work out your salvation with fear and trembling. For God is the one who, for his good purpose, works in you both to desire and to work.'[65] The supernatural merit of good works 'is to be attributed in the first place to the grace of God, then to the faithful. Man's merit, moreover, itself is due to God, for his good actions proceed in Christ, from the predispositions and assistance given by the Holy Spirit'.[66]

When we receive sanctifying grace our nature is lifted up so that we are able to perform meritorious works for life everlasting. In order that our works can be meritorious, it is necessary that we remain united to God through the theological virtue of charity. 'The intensity of the love of God with which an act is performed determines the degree of merit.'[67] To merit eternal life, we must remain united to the supernatural principle of merit which is grace. If we do not remain united to the head, the good works which we perform will not be meritorious, 'just as the branch must remain united to the vine to bear much fruit.'[68] Neither will we have the ability or strength to perform such works unless we are united to God. Fr Avila says that 'the soul is as blind which thinks that its good works come from its own abilities, and not from the supernatural life bestowed on it.'[69] Furthermore, he says, 'Those who imagine they can attain to holiness by any wisdom or strength of their own, will find themselves after many labours, and struggles, and weary efforts, only the farther from possessing it, and this in proportion to their certainty that they of themselves have gained it.'[70] However, the good works which we perform when we are united to God in charity and in a 'state of grace, are of such high value that they are truly just works and merit an increase of our own justice, as Saint John [the Apostle] says "let the one who is just become more just." (Rev 22:11). They are works worthy of attaining to the kingdom of God.'[71] We should therefore thank God constantly for having given us the grace to be able to choose rightly, and for giving us the 'power to merit by using the grace He has mercifully bestowed on' us.[72]

The Infused Virtues and Seven Gifts of the Holy Spirit

In Baptism, along with sanctifying grace, we receive the infused theological and moral virtues and the seven gifts of the Holy Spirit. Both the virtues and the gifts are habits or dispositions which God infuses into the soul. At the natural level, we can think of habits as stable qualities or dispositions which are not easily changed and are rooted in the soul, in its powers and operations. These habits are acquired by repetitive acts. For example, studying is an activity that can seem arduous in the beginning. Yet, with repetition, our minds can become accustomed to the work of reading and thinking and learning, so that we do those activities with greater ease and facility. Likewise, in the supernatural life of grace, God desires to move us in a way that is not shocking to our system, but 'connatural'—like second nature to us. Therefore, in addition to sanctifying grace, He infuses the virtues and gifts through which our intellect and will can cooperate with the grace of God. These virtues and gifts are so necessary and so beautiful, that Fr Avila describes them as 'fine garments' and jewels with which God adorns our soul in order to restore us and bring us into union with Him.[73]

Just as it is necessary that we have grace to perfect the soul, so also it is necessary that we have the infused habits (virtues and gifts) to perfect our intellect and will. Fr Avila, in his writing, sometimes refers to the intellect and will as faculties and powers[74] within the soul; these terms are often used in theology. Both the intellect and will are powers which we have within the soul and in order that we can act 'in accord with the elevated being of the grace' which God gives us, He also infuses into our soul the virtues and gifts of the Holy Spirit.[75] By doing so as Fr Avila explains 'God enriches the powers of the soul to make them function more effectively.'[76] God gives to the soul something which is above the natural faculties of reason and will. He enlightens our understanding, directs our will, inflames us with love, and gives us 'strength to love Him.'[77] Therefore, with sanctifying grace as the principle, and the virtues and gifts of the Holy Spirit as supernatural operative habits, we have what is called the supernatural organism.[78] Sanctifying grace perfects the soul and the infused virtues and gifts perfect the powers of the soul in 'reference to their actions.'[79] Thus by the light of God's grace a person is perfected so that he or she can perform great acts of virtue and love God above all things.[80] It is by being in a state of grace that we can perform actions which are supernatural, for grace is a participation in the life of God. Grace is the very principle of meritorious works through the intermediary of the virtues.[81]

The Difference Between the Virtues and the Gifts

Both the supernatural virtues and the seven gifts of the Holy Spirit are infused into the soul, along with sanctifying grace. Both remain in the soul as long as a person is in a state of grace. Hence, both the virtues and the seven gifts of the Holy Spirit are habits which abide in the soul and in this way, they are similar. However, there is a great difference between the virtues and the gifts and this difference lies in the way in which they are moved. When a person operates or acts through the virtues, it is human reason (aided by faith and grace) which has commanded the act. The infused virtues are like our supernatural God-given muscles. They grow with repetitive acts, each of which is commanded by the graced soul. On the other hand, if a person is operating with the help of one of the seven gifts, it the Holy Spirit Who has moved the person to act;[82] nevertheless, God moves us in a way that is both meritorious and free since the person retains the freedom to accept or reject the prompting of the Holy Spirit.[83]

The difference between the virtues and the gifts can be compared to a sailboat which is moved in different ways. The boat represents the soul. The boat is equipped with oars (representing the virtues) and a sail (representing the gifts). Without any wind, the sailboat must be moved by an oarsman—it is difficult and takes a lot of effort. This is the work of the virtues. However, when a favourable wind comes along, the wind catches the sail and quickly takes the boat to its destination with ease and very little effort.[84] The exercise of rowing represents a person who is functioning with the operation of the virtues, in which the work is difficult and needs the help of the gifts. The wind represents the movement of the Holy Spirit and the sail is the gifts. The sail is only effective in moving the boat when the wind blows. Likewise, the gifts operate when the Holy Spirit chooses.

The *Catechism of the Catholic Church* says that the seven gifts of the Holy Spirit 'complete and perfect the virtues'[85] The infused virtues are something which are supernatural in that they spring from the life of grace; however, we can say that the seven gifts of the Holy Spirit are doubly supernatural due to the fact that they are prompted by the Holy Spirit.[86] The movement of the soul toward union with God through the use of the virtues is slow and arduous because action through the virtues is always according to a human mode. In other words, what we can accomplish through the virtues (even with the help of grace) is limited by our own human capacities. We can imagine the effort required to row the boat against a strong current. Because of these limitations and arduousness, God infuses the gifts. Since the gifts operate at the command of God, their operation is not limited by our human frailty. Thus, as we virtuously row toward union with our Saviour, the wind of the Holy Spirit catches the sail and propels us with ease and efficiency into the heart of Christ.

The Difference Between the Seven Gifts of the Holy Spirit and the Charisms

There is an important difference between the seven gifts of the Holy Spirit and the charisms (or charismatic gifts). The seven gifts of the Holy Spirit are enumerated in Isaiah:

> And the spirit of the Lord shall rest upon Him: the spirit of wisdom, and of understanding, the spirit of counsel, and fortitude, the spirit of knowledge, and of godliness, and He shall be filled with the spirit of the fear of the Lord.[87]

The charismatic gifts are enumerated in 1 Co 12:7–11:

> Now to each one the manifestation of the Spirit
> is given for the common good. To one there is
> given through the Spirit a message of wisdom,
> to another a message of knowledge by means
> of the same Spirit, to another faith by the same
> Spirit, to another gifts of healing by that one
> Spirit, to another miraculous powers, to another
> prophecy, to another distinguishing between
> spirits, to another speaking in different kinds
> of tongues, and to still another the interpreta-
> tion of tongues. All these are the work of one
> and the same Spirit, and he distributes them to
> each one, just as he determines.

The seven gifts of the Holy Spirit are permanent habits which remain in the soul as long as a person remains in the state of grace. On the other hand, the charismatic gifts are not permanent; they are transient graces which God gives from time to time, and hence they do not reside in the soul as habits. The charismatic gifts are for the building up of the body of the church[88] and not directly sanctifying for the person who manifests these graces. On the other hand, the seven gifts of the Holy Spirit are highly sanctifying for the soul in which they are working, and it is absolutely necessary that a person be in a state of grace for these gifts to operate. Nevertheless, when one of the seven gifts is working, it does not necessarily attract attention, and therefore the operation of these gifts often goes unnoticed even by the soul in whom the gifts are working. One sure sign that the gifts are highly operative in a person's soul is a high degree of virtue, because the seven gifts of the Holy Spirit perfect the supernatural virtues.

When one of the charisms is working, a person is not necessarily in a state of grace; sanctifying grace is not absolutely required for the operation of the charismatic gifts. This may come as a surprise since the manifestation of the charisms often seems very impressive; but the working of one or a number of the charismatic gifts is not necessarily indicative of sanctity. In fact, the charismatic gifts can even operate in a person who is in a state of mortal sin. Therefore, if we posses any of the charisms, we should not let this be an occasion for pride. True holiness is always manifested through works of virtue and humility. Fr Avila makes the point that if we find ourselves to be so prideful that we believe ourselves to be better than others, we ought to consider that one person can be less good than another and yet have the gift of prophecy, healing the sick, and similar gifts that are lacking in one who is better than him.[89] St Paul affirms that without charity and grace, we cannot profit even from these impressive charismatic gifts: 'If I speak with the tongues of men and of angels, but do not have love, I have become a noisy gong or a clanging cymbal. If I have the gift of prophecy, and know all mysteries and all knowledge; and if I have all faith, so as to move mountains, but do not have love, I am nothing.'[90]

Pray Often for the Grace of the Holy Spirit

We should pray often for the grace of the Holy Spirit and for an increase in the operation of the seven gifts. St Paul reminds us that 'the love of God has been poured out into our hearts through the Holy Spirit'.[91] In Baptism, we receive the indwelling of the Holy Spirit. 'The same Spirit gives Himself more abundantly in Confirmation, strengthening and confirming Christian life.'[92] The Holy Spirit is the Lord, the Giver of Life, our Advocate, Paraclete, Consoler, and Guide. 'He not only brings to us His divine gifts, but is the Author of them and is Himself the supreme Gift, who, proceeding from the mutual love of the Father and the Son, is justly believed to be and is called "Gift of God most High"'.[93]

Let us pray with St John of Avila: 'May the Holy Ghost, through the merits of Jesus Christ and the blood He shed for us on the Cross, deign to come to our hearts and cure our souls. May He enlighten our understanding so that we may come to know God [and] may He make us will to love only God.'[94] And let us pray with the Universal Church:

> Come, Holy Spirit, and send forth from heaven the ray of your light.
> Come, Father of the poor, come, giver of gifts, come, light of hearts.
> Best Consoler, sweet guest of the soul, sweet coolness.
> Our rest in labour, our shield from the heat, our solace in grief.
> O most blessed light, fill the inmost hearts of your faithful ones.
> Without your grace, there is nothing in man, nothing that is innocent.
> Cleanse what is dirty, moisten what is dry, heal what is wounded.
> Bend what is rigid, warm what is cold, make right what has strayed.
> Grant to your faithful, those who trust in you, the seven-fold gift.
> Grant the reward of virtue, grant the deliverance of salvation, grant everlasting joy.
> Amen. Alleluia.[95]

Notes

1   Longaro degli Oddi, *Life of the Blessed Master John of Avila; Secular Priest, Called the Apostle of Andulusia* (London: Burns and Oates, 1898), p. 51.

2   Oddi, *Life of the Blessed Master John of Avila,* p. 57.

3   The word 'grace' can be understood as a participation in the divine life. See Thomas Aquinas, *Summa Theologiae,* translated by the Fathers of the English Dominican Province (New York. Benziger Brothers, 1948), I–II, q. 110, a. 3, and 2 P 1:4. (*Summa Theologiae* hereafter cited as *ST.*)

4   *ST,* I–II, q. 109, a. 3.

5   John of Avila, *The Holy Ghost,* translated by Ena Dargan (Dublin: Scepter Limited, 1959), III, pp. 59–60 (Hereafter cited as *HG.*)

6   *HG,* VI, p. 128.

7   *ST,* I, q. 95, a. 1.

8   *HG,* III, pp. 60–61.

9   John of Avila, *Audi, Filia—Listen, O Daughter,* translated and introduced by Joan Frances Gormley (New York: Paulist Press, 2006), ch. 1, p. 42. (Hereafter cited as *AF.*)

10 Gn 3:3–4.

11 *HG,* III, pp. 60–61.

12 *HG,* III, p. 60. See *AF* ch. 13, p. 68: John of Avila would explain that because they did not obey God, Who is their superior, their flesh would now rebel against its superior which is reason.

13 *AF,* ch. 86, p. 248.

14 *AF,* ch. 106, p. 299. See Lam 4:8.

15 *ST,* I–II, q. 109, a. 3.

16 See Mt 18:14.

17 *AF,* ch. 86, p. 248.

18 *HG,* III, p. 58.

19 *AF,* ch. 11, p. 64.

20 *ST,* I–II, q. 109, a. 5.

21 *ST,* I–II, q. 112, a. 1.

22 John of Avila, *Letters of Blessed John of Avila,* translated and selected from the Spanish by the Benedictines of Stanbrook (London: Burns & Oates Ltd., 1904), XIX, p. 121. (Hereafter cited as *Letters.*)

23 *ST,* I–II, q. 110, a. 1.

24 *AF,* ch. 112, p. 313.

25   Adolphe Tanquerey, *The Spiritual Life* (New York: Desclee and Co., 1930), pp. 55–56.

26   Servais Pinckaers, *Sources of Christian Ethics*, translated from the third edition by Sr Mary Thomas Noble (Edinburgh: T&T Clark, 1995), p. 453.

27   *Catechism of the Catholic Church*, 1213. (Hereafter cited as *CCC*.)

28   *AF*, ch. 84, p. 241; *AF*, ch. 37, p. 124; *AF*, ch. 11, p. 64.

29   *AF*, ch. 65, p. 193; St Thomas Aquinas, *The Light of Faith: The Compendium of Theology*, translated by Cyril Vollert (Manchester, NH: Sophia Institute Press, 1993), pp. 162–163: 'God's love is the cause of goodness in things and is not called forth by any pre-existing goodness, as our love is.'

30   *AF*, ch. 84, pp. 241–242.

31   *CCC* 1266.

32   Heb 11:1.

33   *AF*, ch. 31, p. 112.

34   1Tm 6:16.

35   *AF*, ch. 31, p. 113.

36   *AF*, ch. 43, p. 134.

37   *Ibid.*, p. 136.

38   *Ibid.*

39   *AF*, ch. 32, p. 114.

40   *Letters*, XXII, p. 142.

41   *AF*, ch. 43, p. 136.

42   *Ibid.*, p. 135.

43   *Ibid.*, p. 136.

44   *AF*, ch. 44, p. 138.

45   *Ibid.*

46   Ph 2:12.

47   *AF*, ch. 44, p. 138.

48   Pope Benedict XVI, *Spe Salvi*, 27.

49   Antonio Royo and Jordan Aumann, *The Theology of Christian Perfection* (Dubuque, IA: The Priory Press, 1962), p. 386.

50   *AF*, ch. 29, p. 103.

51   *CCC* 1818.

52   *CCC* 1817.

53   Pope Benedict XVI, *Deus Caritas Est,* 39.

54   1Jn 4:16.

55   *CCC* 1822.

56   *ST,* II–II, q. 23, a. 1.

57   *AF,* ch. 86, p. 248.

58   *HG,* III, p. 59.

59   Gabriel of St Mary Magdalen, *Divine Intimacy,* translated from the 7th Italian Edition by the Discalced Carmelite Nuns of Boston (Boston: Msgr Wm. J. Doheny,1981), pp. 750 –751. See Jn 15:14, 14:23.

60   Gabriel of St Mary Magdalen, *Divine Intimacy,* pp. 750 –751.

61   See *CCC* 2006.

62   *ST,* I–II, q. 114, prologue.

63   Royo and Aumann, *Theology of Christian Perfection,* p. 107.

64   *CCC* 2008.

65   Ph 2:12–13.

66   *CCC* 2008.

67   Royo and Aumann, *Theology of Christian Perfection,* p. 108.

68   *AF,* ch. 84, pp. 241–242.

69   *Letters,* XXIII, p. 153.

70   *Letters,* XIX, p. 121.

71   *AF,* ch. 84, p. 241.

72   *Letters,* XXIII, p. 151.

73   *HG,* VI, pp. 149–150.

74   *AF,* ch. 66, p. 194.

75   *AF,* ch. 84, p. 241.

76   *HG,* V, p. 119.

77   *HG,* V, p. 120.

78   Reginald Garrigou-Lagrange, *The Three Ages of the Interior Life,* vol. I, translated by Sister M. Timothea Doyle (Rockford, IL: Tan Books and Publishers, Inc., 1989), p. 51.

79   *ST,* III, q. 62, a. 2.

80   Aquinas, *Comp. Theol.,* 162–163.

81   *ST,* I–II, q. 110, a. 4, ad 2.

82   *ST,* II–II, q. 52, a. 2, ad 1.

83   Royo and Aumann, *Theology of Christian Perfection,* p. 87.

84   Marie-Eugène of the Child Jesus, *I Want to See God*, vol. I (Notre Dame, IN: Christian Classics, 1953), p. 339.

85   *CCC* 1831.

86   Reginald Garrigou-Lagrange, *Christian Perfection and Contemplation*, translated by Sister M. Timothea Doyle (Rockford, IL: Tan Books and Publishers, Inc., 2003), p. 38 .

87   Is 11:2–3. *Douay Rheims Catholic Bible*. This translation has been used here because the words used to signify the gifts of the Holy Spirit most closely resemble the words use in the *Catechism of the Catholic Church*, 1831. Garrigou-Lagrange explains that the 'Hebrew text does not mention the gift of piety, but the Septuagint and the Vulgate do. Since the third century, tradition affirms this sevenfold number. Moreover, in the Hebrew text of Isaias, fear is named a second time in verse 3, and in the Old Testament the terms "fear of God" and "piety" have almost the same meaning.' Cf. *Three Ages* I, p. 66. See footnote #1.

88   See Ep 4:11–12.

89   *AF*, ch. 54, p. 167.

90   1 Co 13:1–2.

91   Rom 5:5.

92   Pope Leo XIII, *Divinum Illud Munus*, 9.

93   *Ibid*.

94   *HG*, VI, p. 162.

95   Sequence from the Solemnity of Pentecost.

3

PRAYER AND CONTEMPLATION

Speaking to God from the Heart

F R AVILA'S BOOK *Listen O Daughter*, (*Audi Filia*) is full of practical advice on how to pray. John of Avila is a Saint whom God has raised up to be a witness, in his times and also in ours, of how God desires to lead souls to intimate union with Him. Our Saint was inflamed with the love of God and was brought to the heights of perfection. Even though he was a busy diocesan priest, he had an intense prayer life and was given many extraordinary gifts. Master Avila always encouraged people to pray: 'I do not know why we do not all exercise this office, and with diligence. For we may travel now by land and another time by sea, but we always travel in danger of death.'[1] He speaks of an old proverb which says '"If you do not know how to pray, go to sea." The many dangers in which sailors find themselves make them invoke our Lord.'[2]

There are a variety of motives by which we are drawn to pray and there are different reasons why we apply certain methods throughout the day and at various stages in the spiritual life. There are many different forms of prayer—prayers of petition, prayers of thanksgiving, prayers of contrition, prayers of adoration. There is vocal prayer, mental prayer, contemplative prayer; we can contemplate God's Divine Mysteries and adore His Divine presence in the blessed Sacrament. There are numerous and varied ways in which we can pray; however, in general as Fr Avila says prayer is 'that which comes to pass in one's secret conversation with God.'[3] Methods and techniques in prayer can be useful, but what is important is that we pray from the heart and that we are attentive to God. A vibrant prayer life cannot be produced by simply using methods or techniques. We will not progress in the spiritual life if we do not open our hearts to God in prayer and if we do not pay attention to the One with Whom we are speaking. Cold, mechanical prayer and inattentive prayers will not take us very far. If we learn to lift up our mind and heart to the Lord and remain humble before Him and if we are truly trying to live the Gospel message, sooner or later God will draw us into a deep and intimate relationship with Himself.

Our prayers do not have to be eloquent; God is happy with a simple prayer from a sincere heart. Prayer is born of love and desire, and from this we raise our mind and heart to God; it is simply talking with God from the heart. Through prayer, we come to know God better and grow in union with Him. All of us are called to have an intimate friendship with God; it is only God Who can fulfil the deepest longing of the human heart. When we spend time with God, we are changed. There is no greater friend a person can have and no greater benefits which can be received, as when a soul converses with the Lord—spending time with God is always time very well spent.[4]

Prayer is the means by which we come to love God and grow in love and mercy towards our neighbour. In fact, Fr Avila says the only reason a person lacks mercy towards their neighbour is because he or she lacks 'intimate conversation with God'.[5] As we advance in prayer, we advance in all of the virtues and

gifts of the Holy Spirit. St Teresa of Avila says that the intensity of a person's charity coincides with the intensity of his prayer life.[6] The spiritual life—the status of our friendship with God—is never static, but always dynamic. We are always either growing in intimacy or growing apart. It is therefore very important that we always try to remain faithful to prayer and works of charity; if we cooperate with the graces God gives us, we will advance in the spiritual life and continue to grow in union with Him. We will advance in virtue and obtain many fruits from our time well spent in prayer; for as Fr Avila says, 'Just as plowing and sowing are the means to harvest wheat, so prayer is the means to obtain spiritual fruits.' On the other hand, if we do not spend time in prayer, Fr Avila says, 'We ought not to marvel if we harvest so little, since we sow so little prayer.'[7]

The Privilege of Being Able to Speak to God

In his work *Audi Filia*, John of Avila draws our attention to the great privilege God has given us in that we can speak to Him at any time of the day or night. God is waiting for us to speak to Him; He wants to heal our wounds and grant us many gifts. Fr Avila therefore poses the question, why is it that there are so many people who are so slow to take up this offer? Imagine if a King or someone of great esteem were to offer people the opportunity to meet with Him. How many people would flock to meet with such an important man. However, what benefit does this bring? God, on the other hand waits for us and not only invites us to speak to Him, but pleads with us to do so. How great is this Lord and how immense is His love for His children. He waits for us to speak with Him, so that

He can in turn give us heavenly blessings.[8] God is attentive to our prayers, through Christ, 'not only to hear what we say' but 'the Lord hears our prayers, to fulfil them.'[9] Therefore, as Samuel said, '"Speak, Lord, for your servant hears."[10] In the same way the Lord says to us "Speak, servant, for your Lord hears."'[11]

Fr Avila explains that God is always ready to listen to the prayers of His children. It can be a great comfort when we have a friend who is always willing and ready to listen to our problems, both day and night. It is an even greater gift when this close friend never grows tired of helping us; even if he or she can bring us no remedy, the compassion alone brings us great relief. God not only hears our troubles but He has the power to bring healing and comfort to all our sorrows. The Lord always hears and sees the troubles of those in need. He is forever ready to listen to all our needs and He never leaves us, not even for one moment.[12] Prayer is the means by which we can obtain both bodily and spiritual needs from the hand of a loving Father, but He is sometimes not invoked.[13] God wants all of His children to call on Him at all times; He is a refuge in all kinds of difficulties. God in His great goodness desires that all people speak with Him, but how few desire to approach Him, even though He always invites and desires to reward those who speak to Him.[14] Speaking from experience, Fr Avila points out that those who seek the Lord in times of need will often see, that without their knowing how, their 'affairs have succeeded beyond [their] highest expectations'.[15] We can be assured that whenever we open our heart to the Lord, our prayer never goes unanswered. God always answers our prayer in some way, and never refuses the person who searches for Him with a sincere heart.

Petitioning God in Prayer

God gives us many things throughout our lives even without us ever asking for them. Nevertheless, there are certain things which God wants to give us only when we ask for them. He does this for our own good, so that we may gain confidence in having had recourse to Him and in order that we may recognise Him as the author of all our goods.[16] Unfortunately, a lot of people pray only when they are in dire need, or as a last resort when all else has failed. In this way people place their final confidence in God but their first and greatest confidence is in themselves or in some other person.[17] God wants us to place all our confidence in Him and ask Him for all that we need, both temporal and spiritual. When we pray, for example, that God will help us to grow in some particular virtue, this is a very praiseworthy kind of prayer, because it is a good way to ensure that we will do the Lord's will.[18] Fr Avila points out, however, that people rarely pray for their spiritual needs, but they often pray concerning temporal needs. He explains that this is very unfortunate, for God readily hears and answers prayers when they concern our spiritual well being since He is the Divine Physician Who is waiting to heal and sanctify our souls.[19]

Our Saint is in favour of asking for specific things in prayer, whether spiritual or temporal, rather than asking for things in general. He explains that when we pray for a particular need, this can help us to pray with greater fervour and with deeper groaning. He says that 'these are reasons for God to grant easily what is asked'.[20] On the other hand, if we pray for things in a more general way, our prayer may be much more tepid. Therefore, according to Fr Avila, perhaps God

will not grant this prayer because it is made with such
little fervour. Fr Avila comes to this conclusion because
it conforms with Scripture. In the Our Father, God
teaches His children to ask for things in particular, and
when David was in need, he always presented his
particular needs to the Lord. In fact, all the Saints have
prayed this way when they needed something in
particular. Still, it is good for us to be cautious when
we are asking for temporal needs. In this case we
should make our request 'without too much anxiety
and in a way that pleases the Lord'.[21] In other words,
when praying for temporal things we should not pray
with the 'urgency and anxiety that usually springs
from inordinate love'.[22] St Paul reminds us, 'Have no
anxiety at all, but in everything, by prayer and petition,
with thanksgiving, make your requests known to God.
Then the peace of God that surpasses all understanding will guard your hearts and minds in Christ Jesus,'
(Phil 4:6–7).

The Necessity of Prayer for Charitable Works

John of Avila consulted God for everything he did and
relied on Him in all things. It was unthinkable for Fr
Avila to undertake any task without first taking it to
prayer. He knew it was only through prayer that he
would gain the strength and wisdom he needed each
day, and the hours he spent in works of mercy were
only possible because of the grace that God gave him
in prayer.[23] Fr Avila knew that knowledge 'attained in
prayer exceeds that attained through our own reason
and conjectures, as one who goes to something certain
surpasses the one who, as they say, feels his way
along'.[24] Therefore, whenever our Saint was asked to

give any kind of advice, it was only after having consulted the Lord that he would give any kind of answer.[25]

Fr Avila insisted on the necessity of prayer in order to perform charitable works and was well aware that everything he did was a result of God's grace. He had a saying that 'prayer is as necessary to the soul, in order to obtain the grace of God and the Christian virtues, as water is to the earth for the production of fruits'.[26] He explains that it is through prayer that we will acquire the art of 'exercising charity towards our neighbour.'[27] He says, 'As a man who eats well will become weak if he lacks the repose of sleep, and even runs the risk of losing his judgment, so it happens with the one who works well but does not pray. Prayer is for the soul what sleep is for the body'.[28] To forfeit prayer is to neglect the soul, and just as when the body cannot go on when it is neglected of sleep, so the soul without prayer cannot continue in good works. Fr Avila therefore insists that those 'who want to help themselves by carefully doing works pleasing to God, but do not try to pray, are swimming or fighting with only one hand and are walking with only one foot'.[29]

We cannot continue in works of charity without prayer; no one can go on spending themselves without also receiving. It is through prayer that we recover the light and strength of spirit that has been spent in good works.[30] Fr Avila even reminded St John of God of this truth. He recommended that he *not become so concerned with the needs of others, as to forget himself and the need to seek out time for himself so that he could practise his own devotions*.[31] In order for anyone to perform their occupations well, even a great Saint, it is necessary to gain strength of spirit in prayer. Otherwise, instead of performing works with joy, a person will run the risk of going about grumbling and complaining, 'like a heavily loaded cart with squeaky wheels'.[32]

Fr Avila advises that if we want to imitate Christ or the Saints, we should be accustomed to setting time aside for prayer. If we fail to do this, then we can be certain that we will not be able to fulfil the wishes of Christ, who said through St Paul that He wanted us to pray in every place.[33] Fr Avila does, however, explain that if it is the case that a person cannot leave their obligations for a significant period of time, this should not be a cause for worry. The Lord is happy when we diligently fulfil our obligations. We can make the effort to have God present as much as this is possible and do our work cheerfully for the Lord.[34] Fr Avila also explains that those, who are unable to pray because they are sick, should not be anxious, for the Lord sometimes gives more to a person who is sick in bed, than the person that spends many hours in prayer. If we are sick but nevertheless find we are able to do some kind of prayer, then we should do so, as long as this is not to the disadvantage of our health.[35]

Methods and Stages in Prayer

John of Avila had many mystical experiences; yet, he is somewhat reserved when it comes to writing about the more advanced stages of prayer. His book *Audi Filia* focuses much more on the beginning stages of prayer and certain methods which facilitate one's growth in prayer. He does not systematically lay out the various stages of prayer or growth in the spiritual life. Despite Fr Avila's measured approach in regard to the more advanced stages, it does not mean that he was unfamiliar with them; nor does it mean that he did not experience the higher regions of prayer. He would always encourage people to strive for the highest degree of perfection, even as Christ the Divine Teacher instructed us to do in the Sermon on the Mount: 'Be perfect just as your heavenly Father is perfect.'[36] The great Saint and Doctor of the Church Teresa of Avila, who was proclaimed a Doctor precisely because of her teaching on prayer,[37] sought advice from St John of Avila concerning the higher stages of prayer and consulted Fr Avila when she was concerned about whether her spiritual experiences were authentic. When he received an account of St Teresa's spiritual experiences, he was very well prepared in being able to discern and then confirm that her experiences were indeed authentic. Fr Avila's advice came both from his learning and from his firsthand experience. As a busy diocesan priest, he advised beginners and very advanced souls, as well as those who had reached the heights of perfection. As we strive to grow in union with God, we too can benefit from the advice of Master Avila.

When a person desires to grow in intimacy with the Lord, there is a normative path by which the soul progresses. This road on which the soul journeys has been described in detail by the great Doctors of the Church St John of the Cross and St Teresa of Avila. In the beginning, the person engages in more active forms of prayer. The first step is to learn how to meditate. In the Christian tradition, this means focusing the mind on Christ Who is the fullness of the revelation of the Father. With all the distractions of our earthly existence, we need help to stay focused, and this is where meditation comes in. We read a text from Scripture, or focus on an image of the Lord, or read some other book about God, and then think about what we have read or about the image before our eyes. This *thinking* is the beginning of our meditation, or mental prayer. The purpose of this *thinking* is to enkindle in our hearts a deep love and gratitude to God our Saviour and Best Friend. The heart of our meditation is the free conversation that flows from our hearts to the Heart of the Saviour. We then continue in that conversation until we find that we need help again to focus. At this point, we can return to the Scriptures or reading or sacred image we had used before, and begin the process again.

As we engage in this sort of Christian meditation, having a daily heart to heart conversation with Christ, we are able to read less and then even to speak less, just as close friends, once they have gotten to know each other, can enjoy each others' company. As the soul becomes more proficient in this Christ-centered meditation, the person grows in love for God, and this is reflected in the person's whole life. The person becomes more charitable and more generous with the Lord. As the soul continues to grow in even greater intimacy with the Lord, eventually the Lord begins to infuse His light and love into the soul. The soul's experience of prayer becomes less active, more passive and more receptive. This is the normative journey of each soul who wishes to be a true disciple of Jesus.

Meditation

There are many ways in which we can meditate in order to journey towards God. In meditation, the intellect and will focus on some aspect of Divine Revelation, in order to awaken the interior sentiments of love and gratitude toward God. The goal is to promote loving conversation with God. In addition to meditating on Christ's Passion, we can also meditate on the beauty of God's creation or on the favours which God grants. Just as there are different exercises, so too there are diverse people, with different inclinations. Fr Avila explains that it can be very helpful if we are aware of which exercise works best for us and to follow that method. If we do not already know what works for us, we should pray that God will lead us to that which is most beneficial.[38] Fr Avila's preferred method of prayer was meditating on Christ's Passion.

Our Saint encourages the practice of devotional images to help lift up one's mind and heart to the Lord. He explains how beneficial it can be for us to look upon an image of Jesus; the Church uses images of Christ so that something of the greatness that Christ's presence would have had whilst He walked on this earth will be awakened within a person's heart.[39] It is also a good practice, and very beneficial to the soul, to represent the figure of Christ with the imagination. If a painted image of Christ can benefit the soul, so too can an image painted in the imagination — as long as it is used as a step by which we move beyond the image itself. Everything that represents the Lord can be a powerful instrument by which He draws people to Himself. When our Lord walked this earth it was helpful for people to see him with bodily eyes and then 'to be able to look upon him with the spiritual eyes of faith'.[40] This is because the sacred humanity of Christ was 'specially ordered to have a particular efficacy in helping the devout heart to lift itself to spiritual things'.[41] Of course, we can also use a good book which describes the Lord's Passion in order to help us meditate and to help our minds and hearts to be recollected.[42]

In Christian prayer, the term *recollection* refers to the peaceful state in which the senses become less focused on our surroundings, so that the intellect and will can be more attentive to the presence of God within the soul. To be able to pray peacefully and effectively, it is helpful if we learn to become recollected in prayer; in this way, as Fr Avila says, we will be less distracted or lukewarm.[43] He also advises that when we pray, we should not become attached to praying only in one particular kind of place. We should rather be able to recollect ourselves in any kind of place. When we put our trust in God and try not to be attached to praying only in one setting, eventually we find that we can be recollected almost anywhere. We may even be able to maintain a peaceful sense of recollection after leaving our place of prayer. On the contrary, if we are so intent upon recollecting ourselves only in a set location, we may lose this recollection as soon as we leave. Furthermore, we may even find it difficult to recollect in the very place to which we have tied ourselves.[44]

Fr Avila constantly emphasises the need to remain humble before the Lord with simple loving affection. He was well aware that many people do not understand the calm that should accompany prayer and there are too many people who weary themselves, for example when they are trying to meditate on Christ's Passion. Fr Avila therefore says that we 'ought to know that this business is more of the heart than of the head, since love is the purpose of thinking'.[45] He explains that we should try to be more like a child who calmly and attentively listens to his teacher. Many people go to prayer believing that all depends on them and that by their own strength they can accomplish everything. Fr Avila however, strongly recommends that we should not enter into prayer with the idea that everything depends on us. He says this 'method is more appropriate for studying than for praying'. In prayer, 'you must perform your exercise in dependence on the strength of the Lord, who helps you to think'.[46]

We should never think or meditate so much in prayer, to the extent that it causes mental fatigue. If this happens, then it is better to change our method and proceed simply and calmly, asking the Lord to give as He sees fit. Fr Avila insists that too much thinking 'causes dryness in the soul, which usually causes prayer to be abhorred'.[47] Furthermore, when we meditate using a book, we should not read in such a way that we are so absorbed in the activity of reading that we fail to open our minds and hearts to God. Rather the book should serve as something that will 'awaken the soul's appetite and provide material for recollection and prayer.'[48] In any kind of spiritual reading we do—in which we want the Lord to guide us—we should raise our hearts to the Lord, asking Him to speak to us through the words we read to give us their true meaning. This reading does not need to be anything difficult or complicated and there is no need to cover a lot of pages. Whilst reading, we should not be so anxious about the reading that we forget that God is close to us. We should rather read with moderate and peaceful attention so that this reading will not captivate us or prevent us from being attentive to the Lord.[49]

Any kind of exterior devotion, such as vocal prayer or spiritual reading, should serve to awaken one's interior sentiments of love, gratitude, and the ardent desire to follow Christ. We should be on guard so as not to hinder interior devotion by being overly attached to the exterior devotion.[50] Some people, however, may find that even if they try to give themselves to this kind of interior prayer they are left dry and without any devotion. Since they are unable to spend a long period of time in interior prayer, Fr Avila advises them to continue to pray vocally. He recommends that whilst praying this way they should look at an image or read a devotional book about the Passion, even if this is for a brief moment. Many times, by following these steps a person will rise to the exercise of interior reflection.[51]

Moving from Meditation to Contemplation

It sometimes happens that a soul becomes so caught up in the commitment to spend time in actively meditating and trying to converse with the Lord, that there is little room left for flexibility. This can happen because the soul is deeply attached to the method employed during meditation, or because the soul feels lazy when it is not actively and discursively trying to do the work of meditation. St John of Avila stresses the need for leaving room for the Lord to work in different ways. This counsel is particularly important when the Lord intends for the soul to transition from the more active meditation and mental prayer to the more passive and receptive contemplation He may be about to infuse. This beginning stage of infused contemplation is sometimes called (by St Teresa of Avila) the *prayer of quiet,* and the recollection which the Lord helps the souls to have in preparation for the prayer of quiet is referred to as the *prayer of recollection.* Fr Avila emphasises the importance of remaining peaceful in prayer, and the need to become recollected. This is important advice since the 'divine visitor,' as Fr

Avila calls Him, visits hearts where He finds 'peace and quiet.'[52] When a soul is recollected and peaceful, God 'comes more quickly to teach it and give it the *prayer of quiet* than He would through any other method it might use.'[53] If we are used to being quiet and peaceful in prayer and recollection comes to us rather easily, the Lord may bless us with the prayer of quiet. Thus, the prayer of quiet happens after a soul begins to move from a more active stage of prayer to a more passive stage of prayer.

In the beginning stages of the spiritual life, prayer has a lot more to do with our own efforts since it is more active and we are doing most of the work. For example, when we pray vocally, or we meditate upon the life of Christ or God's creation, God always gives us the grace to pray, but prayer at this stage involves predominantly our active effort; we are doing most of the work. For those who are familiar with the works of St Teresa of Avila, this more active type of prayer, happens mostly in the first three mansions of prayer. As a person advances in his or her life of prayer, they move from a more active to a more passive form of prayer. He or she may feel less drawn to meditation, and more inclined to sit in the presence of the Lord, to be quiet and peaceful, rather than working actively with the intellect. Prayer starts to become less discursive and gradually becomes more simple; this can be described as a simple loving gaze upon the Lord. As the palmist says, the one thing we ask, the one thing we seek, is to gaze on the beauty of the Lord (Ps 27:4). Fr Avila suggests that we try to meditate on the Lord's Passion with a quiet and simple gaze, contemplating the Lord's Holy Face and the immense love of His

Most Sacred Heart.[54] In this way, our thoughts may become a simple loving gaze upon Divine truth.

As a soul continues to practice recollection and a more simple type of prayer, God may bless the soul with *infused contemplation*. As mentioned above, the beginning stage of infused contemplation is sometimes called the *prayer of quiet*. There is a type of contemplation in which we can naturally contemplate; it is something that we can accomplish through our own effort, and is therefore referred to as *acquired contemplation*. In acquired contemplation, our thoughts become more focused upon some truth. This kind of contemplation is not restricted to Christians since it is a human activity and does not require grace. Even in the Christian life of prayer, we can naturally contemplate, for example, by first meditating on various traces of God in the universe or by imagining various scenes from the life of Christ, and then allowing our thoughts to become focused on one simple truth. This type of contemplation is something that everyone can do, but this is not the type of contemplation we are concerned with here.

The kind of contemplation we are speaking of—infused contemplation—is supernatural and flows from sanctifying grace. As the name indicates, this contemplation is given (infused) by the Holy Spirit; it is not something we can produce at will, or something we can demand from God—it is a pure gift. This type of prayer can only be experienced by a person who is in the state of grace. Describing infused contemplation, St Teresa of Avila says, 'In prayer we can do something ourselves, with the help of God. In the contemplation I now mentioned, we can do nothing; His Majesty is the one who does everything, for it is His work and above our nature.'[55] She explains that 'this prayer is no longer our work, for it's something very supernatural and something very much beyond our power to acquire by ourselves.'[56] This is the first stages of 'infused' prayer, and the effort in prayer on the part of the soul becomes less. When this happens a person is moving from a more active type of prayer to a more passive kind of prayer. It is something which God gives and the soul receives; when a soul experiences this type of contemplation it may experience a spiritual taste of the Lord and consequently it can say, *Taste and see that the Lord is sweet* (Ps. 34:9).[57]

In this contemplation, God is infusing His light and love into the soul.[58] The soul may experience a strong love for God, or a gentle peace; or the soul may hardly even be aware that it is receiving anything. This contemplation is called 'infused' precisely because God is infusing His light and love into the soul. The Holy Spirit is now doing more of the work, and the soul is doing less—for this reason, the great spiritual writers of our Tradition say that this type of prayer is more about what God does within the soul, rather than what a person can actively do in prayer. Here, we can note that in the Carmelite tradition, whenever the word *contemplation* is used, it refers to this type of 'infused contemplation'; however, other traditions will often add the word 'infused' to make a distinction between infused and acquired contemplation.

Through infused contemplation, God quietly infuses into the soul a loving knowledge of divine things. In fact the soul can understand many things in a short time without any reflection.[59] This knowledge has not been derived from learning or study; rather, it is a knowledge which comes to us through love. Thus, it is a passive kind of knowing which God infuses into the soul. It allows us to know in an instant what before we may have learned through reading and a lot of meditation. Fr Avila explains that the Lord wants to rest in people's hearts and He desires that they may rest in Him, for by doing so the soul will discover certain truths that formerly it did not understand.[60] Infused contemplation has many different degrees, it can be more or less subtle, or very intense when people are very advanced in the spiritual life. This was the case for many of the Saints and this is how some of the Saints, who could not even read, knew the things of God in such a profound way. God communicates to His intimate friends, to those souls that have a certain intimacy with Him and truly love Him. He leads people deeper and deeper into His mysteries. He begins to instruct the soul and to reveal the very depths of His love.

The person who receives this kind of knowledge must be in a state of grace. One who is not in a state of grace can have some knowledge of God, but that knowledge is limited. This light of infused contemplation is not the type of knowledge that people can have who know God by natural knowledge apart from supernatural grace. The great Angelic Doctor of the Church, St Thomas Aquinas, explains that 'knowledge without love does not suffice for God's indwelling, for 1 Jn (4:16) says: "He that abides in love abides in God and God in him." That is why many persons know God either by natural knowledge or by unformed faith, yet God's Spirit does not dwell in them.'[61] Just because a person believes God exists, it does not mean he or she is in a state of grace; likewise just because a person has faith in Christ, it does not necessarily mean that the person is in a state of grace. A person can still have faith, even when 'grace and love have been lost.'[62] Hence, faith is not enough. Only the person who remains in a state of grace has the possibility of experiencing the gift of infused contemplation, for it requires that the soul be united to God. In order for a person to have a loving union with God, he or she must be united to God though sanctifying grace and the theological virtue of charity, which enables the soul to taste of the divine. Thus, a person must be united to God in some way in order to receive the love and knowledge that God gives through infused contemplation. St Thomas Aquinas explains this using the example of a craftsman or an artist: 'The mind of a [person] is not moved by the Holy Ghost, unless in some way it be united to Him: even as the instrument is not moved by the craftsman, unless there by contact or some other kind of union between them.'[63] This union between the soul and God happens through the theological virtues, the highest one being charity.[64] The loving knowledge of infused contemplation depends upon the love of charity and the gifts of the Holy Spirit. This infusion of God's light and love takes place in the normal development of the life of prayer and the journey toward greater intimacy with God. This is the union to which all Christians are called. In other words, this is not an extraordinary gift which is only reserved for a few souls. This infused light and infused love comes to us from the Holy Spirit and from His gifts in order to make us grow in charity.[65]

A Very Important Stage

Sometimes a soul hinders the blessing that God wants to give through this gift of infused contemplation because it does not understand what is happening.

When God wants to bless a soul with this type of prayer, He is giving a great gift. Unfortunately many souls who arrive at this stage do not advance any further in the spiritual life. The experience of infused contemplation is very different from the more discursive form of prayer to which the soul has been accustomed. It is not always easy for us to recognise that God is blessing us with this type of prayer. Consequently, we may try to continue with our usual more active forms of prayer. For example, a person may sense that he or she desires to sit in silence with the Lord without doing any form of active prayer or meditation. However, even if this person prefers just to sit in the presence of the Lord, enjoying the stillness, he or she may think this is laziness due to a lack of understanding. He or she immediately returns to a more active form of prayer, feeling that it is better to rely on this more familiar way. This is unfortunate; for it would be much better if this person were to remain in loving silence before the Lord. Infused prayer has so many benefits. Indeed when God gives a soul the gift of infused contemplation, it can reach the heights of holiness if it cooperates with God's grace and is serious about living the Gospel message.

Another reason a soul may hinder the reception of this gift is that it is so attached to its own method of prayer, that it cannot let go in order to give God room to work. God will not force Himself on a person, He only helps us in so much as we are willing to remain open to His grace. Therefore, He will leave us to continue in our own way if we do not respond to His grace. Fr Avila had the experience of seeing many people attached to their own way of prayer and the fulfilment of their tasks. He explains that there are people who are so 'full of rules for prayer,' that even if they were to believe the Lord wants to lead them a different way, they do not want to be interrupted. But Fr Avila warns that there is 'nothing more contrary to the exercise of prayer than [people who] think they can rule it by their own discretion.'[66] He says, 'Take as quite certain in this matter that the one who benefits more is the one who humbles himself more, perseveres more, and cries out more to the Lord, not the one who knows more rules.'[67] Remaining overly attached to a method of prayer and the consolation of accomplishing the task of prayer can indeed be hindrances on the journey toward God; for He wants souls to advance on the road to holiness, and infused contemplation is something that can help souls grow rapidly in the spiritual life. Therefore, if we feel that God is moving us into a more passive form of prayer it is very important to give God room to work and not force discursive prayer. By the infused grace of God, we will be raised above a more active form of prayer to the prayer of contemplation. Of course this does not mean that one should abandon the divine office or any other prayer obligations one may have; but we should not be so fixed to certain prayer methods when it comes to private times of prayers and devotion.

Humility is essential whenever we pray and in all various forms of prayer. Fr Avila explains that unfortunately by sticking to their own rules people are deprived of the 'humility and simplicity of a child with which they must converse with God.'[68] Humility and simplicity in prayer are extremely important if we want to advance on our spiritual journey, and cooperate with God's grace. When we humble ourselves before God with a childlike simplicity and are not so self-reliant, we can be more disposed to receive God's grace. Furthermore, we are much more likely to cooperate with the grace the Lord wants to give us in prayer. The soul that is more accustomed to relying on God in everything will usually find the transition of moving from an active to a passive prayer much less difficult. When we are aware of our need to depend on God in all things and humble ourselves before God, our hearts are an 'empty vessel into which He can pour the riches of His mercy. It will [be a] place into which the waters of grace may flow, to make it live happily with God, and bring forth much fruit, like a well-watered garden.'[69]

If the Lord blesses a soul with such a wonderful gift and the soul cooperates, then it will flourish in the life of prayer and grow in virtue. If a soul continues on this path it will reach a very high degree of holiness and union with God. The soul should continue to practise even greater humility and take great care not to place itself in 'the occasion of offending God' says St Teresa of Avila. 'I advise them' she continues, about souls that are receiving this gift 'so strongly not to place themselves in the occasions of sin because the devil tries much harder for a soul of this kind than for very many to whom the Lord does not grant these favors. For such a soul can do great harm to the devil by getting others to follow it, and it could be of great benefit to God's Church.'[70]

Recognising the Beginnings of Infused Contemplation

There are some basic signs which manifest that the Lord is moving a person into a more passive form of prayer. It is crucial that a spiritual director has a basic understanding of some of these signs, even if he has not arrived at this stage himself. If the director has an understanding of what happens when a person is moving from a more active form to a more passive form of prayer, then he can be of great help and encouragement to many souls. More often than not, especially in the beginning stages, a person will be unaware that God is trying to lead him or her in this type of prayer. One of the signs that God is beginning to bless a soul with infused contemplation is that it feels it no longer wants to work actively with the intellect, as one does for example in meditative prayer. A person will often feel like just sitting in the presence of the Lord, being still and quiet, and gazing upon the Lord without saying anything—like a married couple who are together but do not need to say anything to each other. They sit in each other's presence, loving each other and feeling quite comfortable with the silence.

There are some souls who may be very eager to receive the prayer of infused contemplation. However, a soul should not entirely cease discursive meditation until it becomes very clear that God is leading it into infused contemplation.[71] As the soul becomes more sure it is receiving infused contemplation and it moves from a more active to a more passive state of prayer, it will be sufficient to say a gentle word to the Lord from time to time and sometimes even this will not be necessary.[72] It is important to be aware that there are some people who are just lukewarm and have no desire to pray actively. It is not usually difficult however, to distinguish the person that is beginning to receive infused contemplation from the person who is lukewarm, for the person who is lukewarm is lax and without solicitude to serve God.[73] Furthermore, this type of prayer is ordinarily given to those who give themselves entirely to God. This does not mean that a person has to become a religious; rather, the person must be serious and sincere in their desire to serve the Lord, and serious about following the way of the Gospel. If a person is committing deliberate sins then it is a sure sign that he or she will not be receiving infused contemplation; for God gives this type of prayer to those Who give their whole heart to Him.

We should not complain that we are not advancing in our lives of prayer if we hold on to certain sins, whatever those sins may be; for as Fr Avila says, 'If we cannot restrain our tongue, or control our bodies and employ them in good works, can we complain that God does not call us to higher things?'[74] Therefore, if we truly desire to receive this gift from the Lord, we should turn away from sin and be faithful to the Gospel. We should give our whole heart to the Lord and try always to do His will. Infused contemplation is not something we can make happen ourselves; however, we can prepare for it by living a holy life, giving ourselves fully to the Lord, and exercising ourselves in true humility before the Lord. Fr Avila is always encouraging souls to live a life of virtue and remain peaceful and humble before the Lord so that in this way they can be prepared for the divine visitor.

Infused Contemplation is Within the Ordinary Development of Grace

All souls can grow in their life of prayer and be open to receive infused contemplation if they are serious about living the Christian life. Infused contemplation is not something extraordinary. It is supernatural, but also within the normal path that leads to perfection and the normal development of our baptismal grace.

This type of prayer is extremely sanctifying to our soul. It helps a soul advance towards union with God, grow in love towards neighbour and excel in all the virtues. Unlike the charismatic gifts which are for the building up of the body of Christ, infused contemplation is directly sanctifying and meritorious for the one who receives it.[75] It is therefore something for which we can all hope. It is not wrong to desire it; indeed, it is of great benefit to the soul. All souls are called to have an intimate relationship with the Lord and grow in union with Him. The Church is very clear on this point. *Lumen Gentium* states that 'all the faithful of Christ of whatever rank or status, are called to the fullness of the Christian life and to the perfection of charity.'[76] God calls people to different vocations; there are many ways the Lord can be served. Some people are called to a more active life, some a more contemplative life. Sometimes God will have a person more active in one period of their life and then more contemplative in another. Whatever our calling, God can lead us in infused contemplation.

God has called each person to a certain state of life. All He asks is that each person do their duty consciously, always doing the best they can. In this is their salvation. One of the tricks of the devil is that he tries to make people who are already living a good life dissatisfied with the state of life to which God has called them. He often works to make people long for something which they cannot have, and as a consequence they have no peace. The Lord leads each soul on its own unique path. God has the perfect journey for each particular soul. The fact that we are not in a contemplative religious order does not mean that we cannot receive infused contemplation. The Lord needs only our hearts and our love and our dedication to whatever it is He has called us; He will do the rest. There is one thing that remains the same for us all and that is charity, which 'is the soul of the holiness to which all are called: it "governs, shapes, and perfects all the means of sanctification"'.[77]

Notes

[1]   John of Avila, *Audi, Filia—Listen, O Daughter*, translated and introduced by Joan Frances Gormley (New York: Paulist Press, 2006), ch. 70, p. 206. (Hereafter cited as *AF*.)

[2]   *Ibid.*

[3]   *Ibid.*, p. 205.

[4]   *Ibid.*, p. 209.

[5]   *Ibid.*

[6]   Antonio Royo, and Jordan Aumann, *The Theology of Christian Perfection* (Dubuque, IA: The Priory Press, 1962), p. 511. This was confirmed by 'Pius X in a letter to the Carmelites in which he stated that the grades of prayer taught by St Teresa represent so many grades of elevation and ascent towards Christian perfection.'

[7]   *AF*, ch. 70, p. 209.

[8]   *Ibid.*, p. 206.

[9]   *AF*, ch. 85, p. 246.

[10] 1 S 3:10.

[11] *AF*, ch. 85, p. 246.

[12] *AF*, ch. 82, p. 236.

[13] *AF*, ch. 70, p. 206.

[14] *Ibid.*

[15] John of Avila, *Letters of Blessed John of Avila*, translated and selected from the Spanish by the Benedictines of Stanbrook (London: Burns & Oates Ltd., 1904), V, p. 53. (Hereafter cited as *Letters*.)

16 Thomas Aquinas, *Summa Theologiae,* translated by the Fathers of the English Dominican Province (New York. Benziger Brothers, 1948), II–II, q. 83, a. 2, ad 3. (*Summa Theologiae* hereafter cited as *ST*.)

17 *AF,* ch. 70, pp. 206–207.

18 *AF,* ch. 102, p. 289.

19 *AF,* ch. 70, p. 206.

20 *AF,* ch. 102, p. 289.

21 *Ibid.*

22 *AF,* ch. 70 , p. 207.

23 Longaro degli Oddi, *Life of the Blessed Master John of Avila; Secular Priest, Called the Apostle of Andulusia* (London: Burns and Oates, 1898), p. 66.

24 *AF,* ch. 70, p. 208.

25 Oddi, *Life of the Blessed Master John of Avila,* p. 66.

26 *Ibid.*

27 *Ibid.*

28 *AF,* ch. 70, pp. 208–209.

29 *Ibid.*

30 *Ibid.*

31 John of Avila, *Certain Selected Spiritual Epistles* (Rouen: John Le Costurier, 1631), 6, p. 46. (Hereafter cited as *Epistles.*)

32 *AF,* ch. 6, p. 53.

33 *AF,* ch. 70, p. 210. See 1Tm 2:8.

34 *AF,* ch. 81, p. 235.

35 *Epistles,* 42, p. 321.

36 Mt 5:48.

37 The section on the 'Life of Prayer' in the *Catechism of the Catholic Church* contains multiple references to St Teresa of Avila's *Complete Works.* Along with the other great Carmelite Doctors, St John of the Cross and St Thérèse of Lisieux, the Church recommends the teaching of St Teresa of Avila as a sure guide for growth in prayer and the spiritual life.

38 *AF,* ch. 81, pp. 234–235.

39 *AF,* ch. 73, p. 213.

40 *Ibid.,* pp. 213–214.

41 *Ibid.*

42 *AF*, ch. 74, p. 214.

43 *Ibid*.

44 *Epistles*, 26. p. 222.

45 *AF*, ch. 75, pp. 216–217, italics in the original text.

46 *AF*, ch. 75, pp. 216–217.

47 *Ibid.*, p. 216.

48 *AF*, ch. 74, p. 214.

49 *AF*, ch. 59, pp. 181–182.

50 *AF*, ch. 75, p. 218.

51 *AF*, ch. 81, p. 235.

52 *AF*, ch. 74, p. 215.

53 Teresa of Avila, *Way of Perfection* in *The Collected Works*, vol. 2, translated by Kieran Kavanaugh and Otilio Rodriguez (Washington, D.C.: ICS Publications, 1980), ch. 28, p. 141. St Teresa addresses the *prayer of quiet* in her work entitled *The Life*, where she speaks of what she calls the second water of grace, which is around the same stage as the fourth mansion. She also explains the prayer of quiet in the fourth mansion of her work *The Interior Castle*.

54 *AF*, ch. 74, p. 215.

55 Teresa of Avila, *Way*, ch. 25, p. 132.

56 *Ibid.*, ch. 31, pp. 155–156.

57 Ps 33:8 Douay Rheims. In more contemporary translations, such as the RSV–CE, this verse is rendered, 'Taste and see that the Lord is good' (Ps 34:8).

58 Reginald Garrigou-Lagrange, *Christian Perfection and Contemplation*, translated by Sister M. Timothea Doyle (Rockford, IL: Tan Books and Publishers, Inc., 2003), p. 316. Garrigou-Lagrange explains that this type of prayer is quite different, here prayer has become passive, God is infusing His Love and light into the soul and hence there, is an 'inspiration and special illumination of the Holy Ghost.'

59 Teresa of Avila, *The Book of Her Life* in *The Collected Works*, vol. 1, translated by Kieran Kavanaugh and Otilio Rodriguez (Washington, D.C.: ICS Publications, 1980), ch. 12, p. 121.

60 *Epistles*, 36, 288.

61 Thomas Aquinas, *Commentary by Saint Thomas Aquinas on the First Epistle to the Corinthians*, translated by Fabian Larcher,

(paragraphs 987–1046 translated by Daniel Keating). http://nvjournal.net/files/Aquinas-Corinthians.pdf, accessed May 21, 2012, 3–3, p. 173.

62 *AF,* ch. 44, pp. 139–140

63 *ST,* I–II, q. 68, a. 4, ad 3.

64 *ST,* I–II, q. 68, a. 4, ad 3.

65 Garrigou-Lagrange, *Christian Perfection and Contemplation,* pp. 243–244.

66 *AF,* ch. 75, p. 218.

67 *Ibid.*

68 *Ibid.*

69 *Letters,* XXIII, p. 152.

70 Teresa of Avila, *The Interior Castle* in *The Collected Works,* vol. II, translated by Kieran Kavanaugh and Otilio Rodriguez (Washington, D.C.: ICS Publications, 1980), IV, ch. 3, pp. 332–333.

71 Royo and Aumann, *Theology of Christian Perfection,* p. 540.

72 Teresa of Avila, *Way,* ch. 31, p. 156.

73 John of the Cross, *Dark Night of the Soul* in *The Collected Works,* translated by Kieran Kavanaugh and Otilio Rodriguez (Washington, D.C.: ICS Publications, 1991), Bk. 1, ch. 9, p. 3.

74 *Letters,* XIX, p. 120.

75 Royo and Aumann, *Theology of Christian Perfection,* pp. 529–530.

76 Vatican II, *Lumen Gentium,* 40.

77 *CCC* 826. See also *Lumen Gentium,* 42.

4

EXPERIENCES AT PRAYER

Taste and See that the Lord is Sweet

S T JOHN OF Avila only makes reference to some of the various and varied experiences a person can have in the higher stages of prayer in his book *Audi Filia*; however, in his correspondence to his spiritual directees, he often refers to certain experiences which can take place when a person is quite advanced in the spiritual life. As the soul grows in prayer, it may have times where God allows it to taste the things of the spirit in a very intense way. Our Saint points out that there are people who 'enjoy interior communication with our Lord, so familiar that it can hardly be believed'.[1] St Teresa of Avila who had written to John of Avila concerning the *Book of Her Life* describes many experiences which she had in the higher stages of infused contemplation. In his letter of response he writes:

> It is unreasonable for anyone to disbelieve these matters because of their sublime nature, or since it appears incredible that a Majesty so exalted should abase Himself to hold such loving intercourse with His creatures. It is written that 'God is love'—and if He is love, He must needs be infinite love and infinite goodness, and it is no wonder that such love and goodness should at times bestow on certain souls an affection which confounds those who do not understand it. Although many know this by faith, yet, unless

they have experienced it themselves, they cannot understand the affectionate, and more than affectionate way, in which God elects to treat some of His creatures. Those who themselves are far from having received favours of this kind, cannot believe God would deal with others in so different a manner. Yet it would be only reasonable to think that such love, a love which fills us with wonder, must come from God, Who is marvellous in His mercies.[2]

As a person advances in the spiritual life he or she gives everything to God. The soul has been purified from unruly passions and has become much more detached from the things of the world. It has grown in union with God, and is much more disposed to receive the influx of God's light and love. Until we have been purged from many vices, as Fr Avila explains, we will not be able to 'advance in the exercise of familiar conversation with the Lord'. Nor will we be able to have the 'sweetest sleep, which is slept peacefully' in God's arms. In fact our Saint is clear that before we experience this sweet repose we will have 'first struggled and conquered' ourselves by many labours. John of Avila explains that this intimate communion with the Lord is one that is 'completely personal, secret, and kept for those to whom the Lord wants to give it, after they have laboured many years and with much love.'[3] This personal and intimate communication takes place through infused contemplation and is called secret because 'the soul neither knows nor understands how this comes to pass and thus calls it secret.'[4] There is another reason why this contemplation is called secret; it is because of the effects which it produces within the soul. These effects are so difficult to describe that there are no adequate words to fully express this wisdom; it can be so 'secret that it is ineffable.'[5]

The soul that has been purified can now experience and taste the things of the Spirit with much more depth and is able to understand the things of God with much more clarity. It has grown so much in its relationship with God, that God begins to reveal His mysteries of love and instructs the soul in the very depth of its being. This does not happen so much in the beginning stages of infused contemplation; rather, God blesses the soul with these experiences in the more advanced stages, when a person has travelled far in the spiritual life and truly loves Him. This intimate communion with the Lord is very sublime. It is not ordinarily given to a person that has not reached a certain intimacy with God. Many of the Saints who had reached the heights of union with God speak of these intimate embraces. These communications from the Lord are not something extraordinary, but a result of the intensification and full flowering of the grace of infused contemplation.

However, even before reaching the higher stages of the spiritual life, if we are sincerely seeking God we are sometimes given certain 'tastes of God'. For example, even in the beginning stages of the spiritual life, God will often give tender feelings of devotion and a certain attraction towards the things of the Spirit, rather than for the things of the world. He gives us these 'tastes' so that we will draw closer to Him. Knowing that we are weak, inclined to delight and rest, and unable to go for a long time without seeking consolations, the Lord sometimes invites souls to Himself by giving certain spiritual delights. He does this so that we do not go searching for delights which are not good for us.[6] For 'just as carnal pleasure makes one lose the taste for and strength of the spirit, so when the spirit has been tasted, the flesh becomes insipid.'[7] Therefore, the Lord says: 'Eat and drink and be inebriated, my beloved friends,' (Sg 5:1). Fr Avila explains that sometimes God attracts people to Himself by delight, for he knows we are 'such good friends of delight'. He exclaims, 'Let no one, then, Lord, find fault with you by saying that you lack goodness to be loved or delight to be enjoyed, and let no one search for pleasing or delightful conversation outside of you.'[8] Moreover, he testifies, 'I have often witnessed, God withdraws people from harmful pleasures, and even from grievous sins, by sending them His sweet consolations. Who shall place limits to God's mercies?'[9]

Unfortunately, many people do not try or do not realise they can have an intimate relationship with God and that God has many gifts to give us. Thus, they do not seek Him with their whole heart. Fr Avila believes the reason why so many people are lukewarm is because they have not 'tasted of God'; they do not know what it means to hunger for God or 'to be filled' by God. Hence, they neither 'hunger for Him, nor... find satisfaction in creatures, but are cold, indifferent, slothful, and faint-hearted, [and] without relish for the things of God.'[10] On the other hand, he says:

> Whoever knows who you are, Lord, will know how you taste. Beyond all understanding is your being, and so too is 'your sweetness, which you have kept hidden for those that fear you' (Ps 30:20), and for those who renounce from the heart the taste of creatures in order to rejoice in you. You are infinite goodness; you are infinite delight.[11]

We should never limit the work that the Holy Spirit can do within the soul, for sometimes when God visits it, the sweetness that is felt can be very great.[12] At times when we are least expecting it, God comes to visit us with His most intimate embrace and 'a tremendous fire of love' sets our 'heart and soul aflame'.[13] This is a gift of the Holy Spirit Who allows the soul to feel an intense love for God and gives us a taste of the divine. We must not become attached to these spiritual feelings or tastes. Our experiences on the spiritual journey are extremely varied. Sometimes God will allow us to feel His presence; and other times, we may feel nothing but dryness and that God is absent. God knows what will benefit each soul at each moment of the spiritual journey. Whenever God gives us any kind of consolation we should accept it with gratitude and humility.[14] However, we ought to pay attention not to become 'attached with inordinate intensity to spiritual pleasures'[15] and spiritual delights since this can stunt our spiritual growth. We should not go to God expecting or desiring 'sweet feelings'. Fr Avila explains that if people would rid themselves of these desires, then 'the devil would not find certain hairs and appetites by which to take hold of their heads and turn them about, thereby harming and even deceiving them.'[16]

We should learn to be content with whatever God sees fit to give us, and always have confidence in Him, for true faith should not require such favours. 'Some take much account of the hours spent in prayer and the sense of sweetness in it, but not of the benefit they derive from it. They think wrongly that one who experiences greater sweetness and spends more hours in prayer is the greater saint. But, in reality, the greatest is the one who, with contempt for himself, has the

greatest charity.'[17] Therefore, if we want to follow the
Lord we should consider nothing great except the
practise of virtue.[18] If God does give some sweet
experiences, this is all well and good. However, this is
not the reason we should seek God; rather we should
seek Him in order to be alone with Him, speak to Him
as a friend and resolve to follow Him whole-heartedly.
We should focus on doing the will of God, practicing
the virtues and bearing daily crosses with much love;
for love does not 'consist in great delight but in
desiring with strong determination to please God in
everything'.[19] If we do not receive sweet favours and
if we go through periods where we experience dryness
in prayer, and no sweetness at all, we should not be
dismayed, but know it is because God intends to bless
us in ways which are unknown to us, and He wants
to purge us from love of self and to exercise our virtue.[20]

Visions and Revelations

Master Avila was very cautious about experiences in
the spiritual life which are classed as extraordinary —
such as visions and revelations. In a letter written to
St Teresa of Avila, he warns her about how discerning
one must be in regard to these kinds of communications, for he knows how easily we can be deceived.
There are many people who will pride themselves on
having received such communications; so, Fr Avila
warns against pride because the prideful person can
very easily be misled. Such experiences are not necessarily a sign of holiness. Moreover, our Saint explains
that because such graces are not given to anyone on
account of a person's 'merits or strength but, one the
contrary, are often given to souls because of their
weakness, they neither necessarily increase sanctity,

nor are always granted to the greatest saints.'[21] True holiness consists in humble love of God and neighbour.[22]

Fr Avila prefers to encourage people to be content with following the ordinary path which leads to salvation. Visions, revelations, and any kind of supernatural experiences which are extraordinary are not necessary for salvation; nor are they necessary in order to reach a high degree of sanctity. Fr Avila encourages the reading of the life of the St Catherine of Siena, not so a person would desire to have her revelations, but so that he or she would imitate her virtues.[23] Extraordinary communications can be more harmful than good if a soul is not humble, cautious and discerning; therefore our Saint recommends that we beg God 'not to allow us to walk by sight, but to defer the revelation of Himself and His Saints until we reach Heaven'.[24] A lively faith is sufficient because it gives us a firmer belief than if we had seen Jesus with our own eyes and had touched Him with our own hands.[25]

Despite the extreme caution Fr Avila recommends concerning extraordinary communications, he is not opposed to them if God wills to grant them. Fr Avila had numerous extraordinary experiences and St Teresa of Avila was advised to send an account of all of her experiences to Fr Avila. St Teresa experienced so many extraordinary favours from God that many people, including Teresa herself, began to wonder if she was being deluded by the devil. The Inquisitor Soto de Salazar, however, assured Teresa that John of Avila had 'so much experience and authority,' that, if John was to approve her book, her mind could 'be set at rest forever.'[26] After reading an account of St Teresa's experiences Fr Avila assured her that her experiences were authentic; nevertheless, he still highlighted the need for continued caution and the need to pray for guidance.[27]

Even if a person's experiences are genuine, there are still many ways in which the devil can work by trying to deceive a person. Sometimes he does this by trying to mimic divine revelations. Fr Avila points out that he does this for two reasons: the first is in order to discredit God's true revelations and another is in order to 'deceive a person under the appearance of good since he is unable to do so in another way.'[28] The devil wants to try to deceive people who are proud; therefore, through various false speeches and sentiments, and by giving false lights to the understanding, he tries to confuse souls. This of course is by God's permission, for the enemy cannot do anything unless God allows it. God sometimes allows the enemy to try us in order 'to exercise in various ways those who serve him with humility and prudence.'[29] John of Avila advises us to be very discerning and not to believe things to be true so readily. We should have deep humility and a holy and reverential fear of God, so that He does not allow us to be deceived. We should also relate what we have experienced to a spiritual director so that we can be instructed and guided in the truth.[30] Fr Avila insists that if we do receive extraordinary communications we should never dwell on these favours with complacency, even if we are certain they are from God. Rather, we should focus on loving God with all our heart. Fr Avila says 'Do not worship any of these visions, but only our Lord Jesus Christ, either in Heaven, or in the Blessed Sacrament.'[31]

Rules for Discernment

Master Avila offers some rules in order for a person to be able to discern whether their spiritual experiences are truly authentic or false. Some of the signs which indicate our experiences are genuine are that we are ashamed of our faults and that we have more reverence for God and a holy and reverential fear of His infinite goodness. We should not have the desire to frivolously tell others about our experiences, nor should we become so occupied in thinking about these experiences that we start to give them a lot of attention. Furthermore, if these experiences come to memory, we should humble ourselves and marvel that such a great and merciful God gives these favours to one who is so unworthy, and we should give all glory to God.[32] The principle rule for discerning whether a person is receiving certain consolations or visions from God is to notice whether these experiences leave us 'more humble than before.'[33] Fr Avila writes:

> However good a thing that happens to you may appear (tears, or consolation, or knowledge of the things of God, or even that you have ascended to the third heaven), if your soul does not remain, in profound humility, do not trust in or receive it. The reason is that, the higher the thing is, the more dangerous it is, and it will cause you a greater fall. Ask God for his grace so that you may know and humble yourself, and above all this, that he grant you what would be most pleasing to him. But, if this is lacking, all the rest, no matter how valuable it may seem, is not gold but tinsel, and is not flour that sustains but ashes without substance. Pride has this evil, that it despoils the soul of the true

> grace of God. If it leaves any of its goods, they
> are falsified so that they do not please God and
> are the occasion for a greater fall for the one that
> possesses them.[34]

Furthermore, whatever communications we receive
they must be in conformity with the teaching of the
Church.

> Therefore, against this church, let no revelation
> move you or any sentiment of spirit or anything
> greater or less, even if it should appear that the
> one who speaks against her is 'an angel from
> heaven' (cf. Gal 1:8). For it is not possible that
> this would be the truth... Close your ears, then,
> to all doctrine alien to that of the church and
> follow the faith practiced and preserved for
> such a multitude of years...[35]

We should not condemn these favours immediately if
the person does not strike us as particularly holy or
advanced in prayer.[36] Holiness is not a prerequisite for
the reception of such extraordinary divine communications. Nevertheless, in regard to the experiences
which have already occurred, if they are truly authentic, the soul will usually be 'filled with divine understanding' and have 'truth and humility as its most
evident signs.' Fr Avila explains that 'if these two are
joined perfectly in a soul, it is well-known that they
give testimony of the presence of the Holy Spirit'.[37]

On the other hand, if the experiences are from the
deceitful enemy, the effects will be very different. First
of all, the soul will have a desire to relate all its
experiences to others and will have esteem for its own
judgment. It will think that 'God is going to do great
things in and through it'. It will not want to be
corrected and will constantly talk of its experience

turning it over and over in its memory. This deceived soul, will also have the desire that other people talk of its experience. Fr Avila warns, 'When you see these and other signs that demonstrate frivolity of heart, you can say without doubt that the spirit of the demon is walking there.'[38] There are others who believe that God has given them so much light that not only do they believe that they can direct others, they even believe that they can direct themselves and therefore they do not need anyone else's help. These kinds of people are usually friends to all their own opinions and may even have little regard to what the Saints of the Church have said. Assuming that they are directed by God, they wrongly believe that they do not need any other counsel; since they are convinced that God teaches them, they have great certainty about what they think they have been taught.[39]

Do Not Desire Visions

Even though John of Avila emphasises that we should be discerning in all the various communications which we receive from God, he singles out the need to be particularly cautious with visions. He warns, 'Visions, whether imaginary or corporeal, are the most deceptive: they are never to be desired.'[40] Imaginative visions are produced supernaturally in the imagination. They are presented to us with 'as much clarity as are externally existing objects in the physical order.'[41] Corporeal visions—or in other words 'apparitions'— are visions in which spiritual objects are seen with the bodily eyes; these are objects which would normally be invisible to the sense of sight.[42] It is difficult to verify the authenticity of both imaginary and corporeal visions. There is always the possibility that they are influenced by the enemy. Sometimes the only criterion for judgment is 'the fruits or effects which the visions cause in the visionary.'[43] As Jesus Himself says, 'You will know them by their fruits,' (Mt 7:16). It is no wonder that Fr Avila says these visions 'are never to be desired', and why he advises so strongly that we desire to follow the 'common path'.[44] He says, 'Genuine faith believes without the need of argument or miracles ... Let us not ask for any signs of God's favour, but obey His command to rely implicitly on Him, and all will be well with us.'[45]

Spiritual Direction

Fr Avila advises that it is imperative to have a good spiritual director if we are receiving visions. This rule should always be applied because no one should be their own guide. Fr Avila is certain that people who follow this rule have no reason to fear they will be deceived. God will not let anyone be deceived, who with all humility acknowledges that he or she is incompetent to judge these matters without help.[46] Therefore, if we seek guidance from another, and the experiences we are receiving are not from God, they will flee. 'God is a great friend of humility and peace', and the person who seeks counsel is very wise. Indeed, as St Thomas Aquinas teaches, one of the effects of the gift of wisdom—one of the seven gifts of the Holy Spirit—is that it makes us open and docile to receiving counsel from others. Fr Avila says of this gift that 'according to Saint James, [wisdom] "allows itself to be persuaded."'[47] Thus, the person who receives any kind of private revelation from God should seek advice in all humility from a wise spiritual director.[48]

Of course spiritual direction is helpful to everyone; it is not just necessary for those who are having visions or private revelations. Fr Avila recommends that all souls wanting to advance in the spiritual life should have a spiritual director and that if possible it should be someone who is 'learned and experienced in the things of God'.[49] Master Avila cautions his reader against uneducated and inexperienced spiritual directors saying that sometimes they do not have much desire for God or to be illuminated by Him. They often believe something which is truly a gift from the Lord is a deception, and they condemn everything as evil. This is because these things are unknown to them and they can hardly believe such things could take place, other than what takes place within their own hearts. The result is that they give the wrong advice, and end up burdening the directee with excessive fears.[50]

Some spiritual directors may be experienced in the things of devotion, but they have no learning. They may ask a lot of questions and when someone tells them about their experiences, they listen with admiration. Furthermore, the more experiences the directee has, the holier they consider this person to be. They readily approve such experiences as if everything is safe. Due to their ignorance, they often fall into error and may lead people astray. They fail to warn their directees about the cunning of the evil one. Both of these types of directors—the one who thinks that nothing is from God which is outside his own limited experience, and the one who thinks every experience is from God—are not fit to be giving good spiritual advice.[51]

A good spiritual director is experienced in spiritual matters, and his judgment is very good. This kind of spiritual director knows the questions which he should ask and with how much caution he must proceed. A person with these qualities understands that true sanctity consists in fulfilling the will of the Lord, not in the amount of experiences one receives. This is the mark of a good spiritual director and someone that can be trusted.[52]

Intrusive Images in Prayer

One may have varied experiences in prayer—very sweet and delightful consolations, and favours and revelations from God, or difficult experiences which can disturb us if we do not understand what is happening. When we begin to develop the habit of prayer the enemy always wants to put an end to it. St John of Avila has a lot of insight about how the enemy can try to distract us in prayer. He warns beginners by explaining that 'the devil particularly tries to trouble them with impure images at the time of prayer'.[53]

This evil tactic can cause a lot of havoc for the person who does not have someone to explain what is happening.[54] 'At times, these thoughts are so many and so terrible that the person never heard, knew, or thought of the kinds of things that come to [the] imagination.'[55]As a consequence the soul becomes very anxious, believing such images come from its own imagination. This in turn causes great disturbance to prayer and sometimes makes the poor soul abandon prayer altogether. Of course, this is exactly what the devil wants.[56] One way to know if these foul images are indeed from the devil is that they will usually come very suddenly and at a time when we least want them, and when 'there is least motive for them'—for example, when we are at Mass or at prayer, and in various sacred places.[57] Fr Avila advises that if we think these impure images could tempt us in any way we should do all we can to pray vocally in order to distract ourselves and take our mind off these images. We should do all that is possible not to abandon prayer and ask the Lord to help us; if we do this, we will end the time of prayer well.[58]

We should try never to become discouraged if we are assailed with such thoughts, for according to Fr Avila, this persecution the devil is waging is a sign that our prayer is advantageous. We should hold fast and not lose strength in this fight; when the Lord sees that it is better that such thoughts cease, He will with pity and with power command our enemy to be quiet. Consequently the conversation we are used to having with God can continue.[59] Finally, if these intrusive images also come outside of prayer, it is good to be engaged in some kind of work that requires attention and effort, so that the images can be forgotten.[60]

Blasphemous Thoughts

Bad images are not the only tactic the enemy uses to disturb a person's prayer. Sometimes he will try to discourage us by bringing to our mind thoughts which are against faith or abominable thoughts against the things of God. We may think these thoughts originate from our own imagination and that we have consented to them, but this is not true. The demon, knowing we are not going to consent to such thoughts, makes it his chief intent to discourage us. If we know little or nothing about the tricks of the enemy, we can become so worn out that we become despondent and agitated. Fr Avila explains that people will often be distracted in prayer and try to make the thoughts go away by swatting them like flies. They think they have consented to the thoughts and do not realise that there is 'a great deal of difference between sensing them and consenting to them.'[61] However, these are the works of the devil and the words and images which he pretends are our own. The soul who undergoes such trials has no cause for scruple; it has not sinned. It has no part in it, for it desires no such thought; the devil merely torments it in this way. If a spiritual director or a very good friend truly knows this soul, they will know its conscience well. They will be able to help it understand that it has not given consent and that it is only fear which makes it think so.[62]

John of Avila's Advice

Our Saint comments that some people say, 'These bad thoughts take away my devotion, and they usually come to me when I approach devotion and good works. Sometimes they make me feel like stopping the good that I have started so that I do not hear such things.'[63] This is exactly what the enemy wants. Fr Avila advises that when these bad thoughts come, the best remedy is to remain calm. We should act as if we do not notice these thoughts and try not to become disheartened or discouraged.[64] It is best to act as if these thoughts or words belong to another, for even though it may cause us pain to hear God blasphemed, in a certain respect, it would bring us some comfort to see that we are not the one who causes the offence.[65] However, all of this is not sufficient unless we put all our hope in the Lord and call upon Him. We must not listen to the lies of the enemy; instead, we should unite ourselves with God. The more horrible the thoughts, the more we should confide in the Lord. He will always protect those who confide in Him, and who have no inclination towards such thoughts but only horror. Fr Avila recommends that we say many times throughout the day 'we believe what our holy mother the church believes, and that it is not our will to consent to false or foul thoughts. We must say to the Lord what is written, "Lord I suffer violence, answer for me" (Isa 38:14), and trust in his mercy that he will do so.'[66]

We must not allow these thoughts to influence us so strongly that we lose time in prayer or cease continuing in any good we were doing. Therefore, even if the enemy circles around us giving us all kinds of thoughts, instead of decreasing in the good, we should deliberately increase it. In this way where the demon thought he could gain, he instead goes away with a loss. There is nothing more annoying to the enemy than a person who pays no attention to such thoughts. Finally, we should not try to reason about such things, for there is nothing so dangerous as to give 'reasons to one who can so quickly deceive us'.[67] Moreover, if we are always trying to reason everything out and give answers, our Saint asks, 'How are we to ask God to respond for us? "Be silent," scripture says, "and the Lord will fight for you" (Ex 14:14).'[68] Fr Avila explains to all who are afflicted with such trials:

> By keeping quiet, by dissimulation, and by hope, I have seen many persons healed in a short time from this painful disease. They have silenced the demon by letting him see that they were not listening or responding to him. It is as puppies that bark usually do. If a man passes by quietly, they are also quiet. Otherwise, they bark all the more.[69]

Merits and Benefits Gained

Many souls are challenged by intrusive images and blasphemous thoughts. It is important to remember that God sees the heart very clearly; He knows when a person is a lover of His ways. Even though these trials can be disturbing, we will not be worse off for having had these experiences.[70] The merits and benefits which we will draw from these hardships are much greater than the conflict we suffer.[71] Through such an experience, we come to know our true weakness and have less esteem for ourselves. This trial should help draw us closer to God and give us much greater trust and confidence in Him. It should help us to see that only God can deliver us from such trouble. We learn about the malice of the enemy and how to discern his wicked ways and escape from his snares; for we will have learnt by experience how to discern things which are discerned by few people.[72] We therefore gain a lot in these wars against the enemy, and the Lord draws many fruits from these difficult encounters. Even though the enemy was hoping to gain by pretending to have made us fall, he loses and is put to scorn, 'whilst we profit, and purify our souls by that very means, which he used, for the disadvantage thereof'.[73]

Notes

[1] John of Avila, *Audi, Filia — Listen, O Daughter,* translated and introduced by Joan Frances Gormley (New York: Paulist Press, 2006), ch. 17, p. 77. (Hereafter cited as *AF.*)

[2] John of Avila, *Letters of Blessed John of Avila,* translated and selected from the Spanish by the Benedictines of Stanbrook (London: Burns & Oates Ltd., 1904), I, p. 21. (Hereafter cited as *Letters.*)

[3] *AF,* ch. 77, pp. 224–225.

4   John of the Cross, *Dark Night of the Soul* in *The Collected Works*, translated by Kieran Kavanaugh and Otilio Rodriguez (Washington, D.C.: ICS Publications, 1991), Bk. II, ch.17, p. 368.

5   John of the Cross, *Dark Night*, Bk. II, ch. 17, pp. 368–369.

6   *AF*, ch. 9, p. 59

7   *Ibid.*, p. 58.

8   *Ibid.*, p. 59.

9   *Letters*, I, p. 20.

10 E. Allison Peers, *The Mystics of Spain* (New York: Dover Publications Inc., 2002), p. 72.

11 *AF*, ch. 9, p. 59.

12 *Ibid.*, p. 58.

13 John of Avila, *The Holy Ghost*, translated by Ena Dargan (Dublin: Scepter Limited, 1959), V, p. 123. (Hereafter cited as *HG*.)

14 *AF*, ch. 13, p. 68.

15 *Ibid.*, p. 98.

16 *AF*, ch. 26, p. 97.

17 *AF*, ch. 76, p. 219.

18 *AF*, ch. 3, p. 44.

19 Teresa of Avila, *The Interior Castle* in *The Collected Works*, vol. II, translated by Kieran Kavanaugh and Otilio Rodriguez (Washington, D.C.: ICS Publications, 1980), IV, ch. 1, p. 328.

20 John of Avila, *Certain Selected Spiritual Epistles* (Rouen: John Le Costurier, 1631), 36, pp. 283–284. (Hereafter cited as *Epistles*.)

21 *Letters*, I, pp. 19–21.

22 *Ibid.*, p. 22.

23 *AF*, ch. 101, p. 288.

24 *Letters*, I, pp. 19–21.

25 *AF*, ch. 34, p. 134.

26 *Letters*, I, p. 17.

27 *Ibid.*, p. 23.

28 *AF*, ch. 50, p. 157.

29 *AF*, ch. 17, p. 77.

30 *Ibid.*

31 *Letters*, I, p. 22.

32   *AF,* ch. 52, pp. 162–163

33   *Ibid.*

34   *AF,* ch. 52, p. 163.

35   *AF,* ch. 46, p. 148.

36   *Letters,* I, p. 20.

37   *AF,* ch. 52, p. 163.

38   *Ibid.*

39   *AF,* ch. 52, p. 164.

40   *Letters,* I, p. 19.

41   Antonio Royo, and Jordan Aumann, *The Theology of Christian Perfection* (Dubuque, IA: The Priory Press, 1962), p. 655.

42   Royo and Aumann, *Theology of Christian Perfection,* p. 655.

43   *Ibid.,* pp. 657–658

44   *Letters,* I, p. 19–20.

45   *Letters,* XVII, p. 108.

46   *Letters,* I, p. 20.

47   *AF,* ch. 54, p. 167; cf. Jm 3:17.

48   *AF,* ch. 51, p. 161.

49   *AF,* ch. 55, p. 169.

50   *Ibid.*

51   *Ibid.*

52   *Ibid.,* pp. 169–170.

53   *AF,* ch. 6, p. 54.

54   *Ibid.*

55   *AF,* ch. 6, p. 52.

56   *Ibid.,* p. 54.

57   *Ibid.,* p. 52.

58   *Ibid.,* p. 54.

59   *Ibid.*

60   *Ibid.,* p. 53.

61   *AF,* ch. 25, pp. 95–96.

62   *Epistles,* 57, p. 439–440.

63   *AF,* ch. 26, p. 96.

64   *AF,* ch. 25, pp. 95–96.

65   *Epistles,* 57, pp. 439–440.

[66]   *AF,* ch. 25, p. 96.
[67]   *Ibid.,* pp. 95–96.
[68]   *Ibid.,* p. 96.
[69]   *Ibid.*
[70]   *Epistles,* 30, p. 241.
[71]   *Epistles,* 57, p. 439.
[72]   *Epistles,* 30, p. 242.
[73]   *Ibid.,* pp. 242–243.

5

SELF-KNOWLEDGE

The Allurements of the World and the Desire to be Honoured

EFORE WE CAN enter into deep intimate communion with Christ through prayer, we must turn
away from the vanities and allurements of the
world. One of Fr Avila's constant goals was to convince people of the emptiness of the luxuries and
vanities of the world. Our Saint was used to dealing
with people with all kinds of human weaknesses,
struggles and temptations, and this is reflected in his
writing. His teaching was extremely beneficial in his
own time, and is just as relevant for us today. The
world around us is always changing, but the gospel
message remains the same. Fr Avila spares no details
in trying to convince people of the horrors of sin and
the false pleasures of the world. His advice is very
direct and practical, sometimes hard, but nevertheless
filled with a sense of compassion. The many people
who flocked to hear Fr Avila's sermons were often
warned about the false pleasure of the world which he
referred to as 'a golden cup with poison inside that
intoxicates those who look only at external appearance'.[1] In one sermon, he declared, 'You are ready to
lose God for a despicable pleasure that will pass in a
moment.'[2] He said that 'sin to the soul is like pestilence
or arsenic to the body',[3] and he described a person who
believes himself to be just, but is in a state of grave sin,

to be like a person who has leprosy, but considers himself to be healthy.[4] Fr Avila did not hesitate to remind people about the true reality of death—that each person will have to face the Lord and render an account for his life. Here each soul will remember 'the offenses it committed against our Lord in this life. Those that previously seemed light will then seem very grave ... Finally, little by little, the hour will approach in which, at God's command, the soul will leave the body and take upon itself the decision either of eternal perdition or eternal salvation.'[5] This hour of death might not be as easy as one might think, for according to Fr Avila, at the hour of death there 'will be no lack of demons' to accuse us and 'demand God for justice' against our soul, as they accuse us 'individually of each sin.'[6]

In his efforts to turn people away from sin, Fr Avila does not just dwell on the ugliness of sin; he also focuses on the mercy of God and explains that it is only God Who can make a person truly happy. He therefore encourages everyone to keep their eyes fixed on the Lord and speaks of the joy which comes as a result of having an intimate relationship with the Him.[7] Only God can truly satisfy the human heart. We learn from experience that no sooner do we possess something, than we want something else; for as Fr Avila says, 'The joy drawn from creatures is brief, vain, tainted, and mingled with sorrow, because the tree from which it is taken has the same qualities.'[8] However, the joys we can receive from God are 'so worthy of esteem that, if all created joys were joined together, they would truly be bitter gall in comparison'.[9] In a letter to one of his directees, he writes:

> When shall we be moved by truth rather than
> by vanity; by beauty rather than by ugliness; by
> quietness rather than by restlessness; by the
> Creator, so satisfying and all-sufficient, rather
> than by the creature that is poor and empty?
> And who, O Lord, shall open our eyes and
> make us realise that apart from Thee there is
> nothing that can satiate or abide?[10]

Fr Avila explains that in order for us to find true joy
and happiness in the Lord, we must follow Him with
our whole heart. If we give up worldly pleasures with
the desire to do what is right, but remain slothful,
tepid, and without fervour, we will not find happiness
in the things of God. We will rather feel stuck between
the things of the world and the things of God and find
fulfilment in neither.[11] On the other hand, if we follow
the Lord with our whole heart, we will begin to have
a taste for spiritual things rather than the things of the
world; worldly things will seem much less attractive
to us and we will begin to have a passionate love for
God. Fr Avila asks, why is it that so few people seek
the Holy Spirit or never trouble themselves to ask
whether they have the Holy Spirit? People enjoy all
kinds of delights, they worry themselves over worldly
things, but how few there are who really love the Holy
Spirit and desire Him, 'though His rewards are so
much greater than those of the world'.[12] He says that
'if you could see the beauty which the Holy Ghost
brings to the soul where He dwells, you would follow
it enchanted, and all the beauties of this world would
fill you with disgust. When He who created the sun is
in your soul, what must it be like?'[13]

Desire for Honours

Not only must we turn away from the enticements of the world if we want to follow God, we must also be careful to avoid the desire for seeking authority and honours for ourselves. This desire can so completely blind a person that Fr Avila says, 'It causes those who dare not do what is easy and safe to undertake what is full of dangers and difficulty.'[14] He suggests that if we struggle with this temptation, the example of Christ is a wonderful medicine for conquering and uprooting vainglory.[15] Furthermore, we can aim to be more like St Paul, who preferred to be 'despised and dishonoured for the sake of Jesus Christ, whose cross he regarded as the supreme honor (cf. Gal 6:14).'[16] Fr Avila insists that a heart such as this is worthy of trust for it would not undertake any great work unless it were 'necessary for some good end'.[17]

The desire for honour however is not bad in every respect. Fr Avila is careful to make the distinction between seeking honour for oneself and resting in it, 'which is evil', and honour which is for a good end. For example, those who are in a position of authority should desire esteem in the sense that esteem is 'needed to discharge their office for the greater good.'[18] It is very difficult, however, for a person to receive honour without letting it cleave to the heart; it requires great strength and virtue.[19] If we do not have a position of authority, if we do not receive honour, and even if we are in the lowest of places, we should not be dismayed. We need a lot more strength to 'remain virtuous in success and prosperity than in adversity',[20] and more grace is needed to prevent us from falling when we are in an important position than when we are 'brought low by misfortune'. [21]

As Christians, we should desire to glorify God in all that we do. However, we are so prone to self-love that sometimes even when we are acting with the intention of seeking God's glory, we find ourselves looking for our own.[22] We also have a tendency to feel regret if we see others advance more than ourselves in the spiritual life, and this also springs from inordinate self-love. Perfect charity desires only that God be glorified in all things. If we truly desire to see God glorified, we should rejoice at seeing others love and serve God so well. 'The love for God and man, then, both concur to the one end that God may be praised and worshipped.'[23]

Necessity of Humility

The virtue of humility was most dear to John of Avila.[24] His book *Audi Filia* is full of advice concerning the virtue of humility. Fr Avila insists that we must remain humble in order to advance in the spiritual life; for if we do not have humility, we will stray far from the way of perfection.[25] Our Saint says, 'The Son of God came down from heaven and taught us by His life and words the way to heaven, and that way is humility.'[26] Jesus is our most perfect example. He wants us all to understand the importance of humility: 'Learn [from] me, because I am meek and humble of heart.' (Matt 11:29)[27] The Blessed Virgin Mary is our second example of humility; 'she taught Saint Elizabeth and the whole world that no glory was due to her for her greatness but to God. With profound reverence, she began to sing: "My soul magnifies the Lord" (Luke 1:42–46).'[28]

The virtue of humility is a beautiful treasure and essential for growth in the spiritual life. Fr Avila explains that just as a building with a weak and unstable foundation may fall at any moment, so the person without the virtue of humility could be 'knocked down by the wind of pride' at any moment. The virtue of humility is a solid foundation for spiritual growth; without it our good works may be the occasion for loss instead of gain. In order for us to avoid falling into the sin of pride, our humility should be 'in conformity with the loftiness of the virtues.'[29] The more virtuous we are or aspire to be, the more humble we should strive to be. All the Saints exhibited this precious virtue and spoke of the necessity to practice it. The great St Augustine says, 'If you ask me the way to heaven, I will answer that it is humility. If you ask me a third time, I will answer the same, If you ask me a thousand times, I will reply a thousand times that there is no other way than humility.'[30] St John of Avila insists that we follow St Augustine's words of wisdom if we are to advance along the road to perfection, not only to avoid falling into sin, but also because God gives grace to those who are more humble.[31] Fr Avila says, 'be aware that the humble of heart, not the high and mighty, are his dwelling places.'[32]

We must therefore, humble ourselves and be on guard against the entrance of pride. Fr Avila describes the human person as having a secret and deep rooted pride, with a desire to be almost divine. This has been inherited because of the original sin.[33] It 'reaches to our very bones, no human strength suffices to cleanse us completely of this sin.'[34] Fr Avila is aware of the difficulty a person can have in recognizing where their pride lies. He says, pride can be 'so buried in the secret chamber' of a person's heart that it remains hidden.[35] The devil, being well aware of this, wages war against us because he wants to separate us from God.[36] He knows that it was pride that changed him from a holy angel into an ugly demon; so he does all that he can to make us prideful. He does this so that being like him in pride, we will also suffer torment like him. He lays secret traps to deceive people, often by inciting them to have very high thoughts of themselves, so that they will fall into the sin of pride.[37] If we resolve to stay close to God, we must be always watchful. We must live in the truth, and be attentive to how we stand before God; for sometimes the more we esteem ourselves and the greater virtue we believe we have, the worse off we really are.[38]

In the eyes of the world, it is perfectly acceptable and good for people to have complete confidence in themselves and a firm will to procure their own happiness. However, in the eyes of the Lord, such things are offensive, and hinder our friendship and communication with Him.[39] The enemy knows that it is good if he can keep souls thinking in the worldly way. For the enemy, it is even better than if souls were to fall into more apparent sins; for if they were to think their sins are bad, even in the eyes of the world, they would soon amend their ways. Therefore, wishing to keep souls in interior blindness, the enemy does not try to induce souls to commit such apparent sins; if he were to do this, souls would escape from his hands.[40] Fr Avila says, 'He knows very well how displeasing pride is to God, and that by itself, it is enough to render useless everything else that a person may possess, however good it may appear.'[41] Consequently it does not trouble him much to see someone praying, remaining silent, reciting the divine office and like things, because he aims chiefly at the heart, hoping that we will have a vain complacence and inordinate love of ourselves.[42] We must be always on guard because the enemy 'counts it as small loss that someone does something good, as long as he is able to win that person completely by the sin of pride and the other sins that follow in its train'.[43]

Our Saint advises that we should learn how to examine our hearts with the light of truth.[44] It may seem that there is nothing to see, but Fr Avila says, 'Our sins are greater than our human intellect can realise, and only our Creator, who sees to the bottom of the human heart, knows all its weakness, for often that which seems perfect to us is very evil in His sight.'[45] However, God, who discerns the heart, can help us discover our secret hidden pride if we ask Him in prayer; then little by little, with the grace of God, we will see what is in the secret corners of our heart.[46] Self-knowledge is a jewel that helps us come closer to God; if we know ourselves we come to know how much we need God. By knowing ourselves and recognising our unworthiness before Him and His great love for us, deep seated pride can be uprooted and we can avoid becoming even more prideful. We will be more aware that we can do nothing without God and therefore humble ourselves before Him. Humility is fostered by recognizing our own weakness and God's countless gifts. God sustains us in every moment of our lives; if He were to cease protecting us, we would certainly return to the sins from which God had rescued us and we may commit even greater sins.[47] When we learn to be aware of our own weakness, we receive the precious jewel of humility.[48] We should learn to live in the truth, always aware of our weakness, and beg for humility with perseverance, for it is a special gift which God grants to His children.[49]

Do not be Discouraged

In order to help us gain some self-knowledge and recognise our pride and our many other faults, Fr Avila recommends that we reflect on some words from a book of sound doctrine.[50] Most importantly we should ask the Lord to speak to our hearts so that we can understand the words we read; thus, we can feel sorrow for our sin, but also confidence in God's mercy. By reflecting in this way our prayer and reading will go along with each other.[51] If we do not feel any kind of shame or sorrow, we should not be disturbed; rather, we should place ourselves before God, asking Him to show us who we are, and what we should feel about ourselves.[52] We can consider all the virtues that Christ exercised in His most sacred Passion – His charity, His meekness, His patience without end, and His silence. In doing so, all our faults are sure to appear, even if they are most hidden.[53] We can evaluate our faults and present ourselves before the Lord in all humility. Fr Avila explains that there is nothing that moves the heart of God so much as the soul that weighs up its faults and comes before Him with sorrow and self-accusation.[54] As we examine ourselves, we must have great confidence in the bounty and riches of God's mercy.[55] We should not become discouraged or lose hope when we reflect on our faults.[56]

The Scriptures assure us that 'all the ways of the Lord are mercy and truth,' (Ps 24:10). The Lord calls us to live in the truth, but He never desires that we become discouraged by the weight of our sins and failures. Jesus Himself exclaims that He did not come for the righteous, but to seek and save those who have been lost. In the same vein, Master Avila encourages us not to fall into despair or to become overwhelmed by our sins. He says that God is displeased when a sin which is very small is made out to be as big as an elephant, and even more so when that which is not a sin at all, is made out to be a sin; in this way we offend against God's truth.[57] Fr Avila explains that we should never fall into dismay or be too afflicted by the thought of our sins since God 'esteems this to be of more disservice to Him than the very fall itself'.[58] Our Blessed Saviour underwent His Passion and death so that we would never have to despair because of our sins. Despair dishonours God's goodness, for He 'so loved the world that He gave His only Son, that whoever believes in Him should not perish but have eternal life' (Jn 3:16). God calls us to believe in His mercy and trust in His providential love. The Israelites committed many sins in the desert, but God continued to favour them. However, He 'did not tolerate their distrust and despair toward his mercy and power. As David said, "He swore to them in his wrath that they would not enter into his rest." And as he swore, so he fulfilled.'[59] We should not lose hope, for God loves us as we are. We must be content that God's love comes from His sheer Goodness and not because of our merits. By His wounds, Christ gives us grace and supplies for all that is lacking in us, healing us and making us lovely.[60] We must therefore never despair by thinking that redemption is so difficult; no matter how weak we are, it is enough for us 'to direct a heartfelt sigh to God, with sorrow for having offended such a Father and with the intention of amendment.'[61] True faith believes and puts confidence in God's goodness, even when we are inclined to distrust or despair.[62] Our Saint exclaims, 'O God most loving,

Who are Love itself, how we wound Thee if we trust not in Thee with all our hearts!'[63]

We should always trust in the mercy of God and take refuge in the most Sacred Heart of Jesus. Truly, it offends against God's love when we think that He has forgotten us, for we are always in His providential care; and it offends against His mercy not to believe oneself to have been pardoned, when He has already pardoned us.[64] According to Fr Avila, God 'takes more delight and glory, and uses [mercy] more, than in the manifestation of the other attributes.'[65] As the prophet David says, 'His mercies are over all his works.'[66] The Lord is very pleased when we hope in his mercy;[67] moreover, while we hope we cannot despair.[68] Both God's works of love and mercy manifest His goodness.[69] Fr Avila explains that God's love to us, 'is more than wonderful', yet some people are unable to believe it 'in respect that it is so strange a thing'; but this is a great offence to God, for He is infinitely merciful, and there is no limit to His love for us.[70] Our Saint therefore says that two things are most advisable, 'one is, that we should love [God's] goodness, and the second is, that we should trust in His mercy.'[71] Truly, we can have confidence in the Lord's love and mercy and know that He always completes what He has begun in us, insofar as we reverence Him in all humility, holy fear, and complete trust.[72] We can be comforted by the fact that we are forgiven and absolved through the Sacraments and our penances.[73] Our Saint says 'Cast away, then, all doubts, faintheartedness and misgivings, for the merits of the Passion are ours, because Christ gave them to us, and we are His.'[74] Jesus 'conquered sin perfectly, meriting pardon for the sins we had committed and strength not to go on committing them.'[75]

We ought to be aware that the evil one often tries to fire dangerous darts to humiliate and discourage people 'to the point of driving [them] to despair.'[76] He wants to weaken people and pull them down so that they will lose their confidence in God.[77] Sometimes he will bring to mind past sins and try to make us forget we have been forgiven; he may also make us forget the many good works which we have been able to do by the gift of God's grace.[78] At other times he will try to frighten us with the number or greatness of present sins.[79] He may even try to trick us into thinking that we cannot go to communion. However, if we are not consciously aware of any mortal sin we can approach the Sacrament with confidence; we should pray to Jesus on the Cross and know that our Lord waits to bless us through this Sacrament of love.[80]

We never have grounds to lose confidence in the Lord who loves us so much and is full of infinite mercy. He is a God of mercy and also a God of justice, but we can be reassured that God 'does not use the rigor of a judge without having first used the mercy of a Father.'[81] We should have confidence and trust in the Lord, for His mercy is never closed to those who 'desire to take refuge in his merciful heart.'[82] Our Saint declares:

> God is so faithful that He never abandons those who have recourse to Him; His love is so tender that far sooner will the sea run dry, or the sun cease shining, than the heavenly Father lack pity for His own. Therefore do they run and fly because God carries them; they stumble not, for He upholds them; they err not, for He is their

guide, and never will they be condemned, for He gives His kingdom to those who 'become as little children.'[83]

Reflecting on the Lord's Passion

Fr Avila explains, 'It is customary to advise those who are crossing a river to look upward or at least away from the water, lest they should faint when they see the moving stream. Similarly, anyone who feels discouragement at the sight of his sins should raise his eyes to Jesus Christ on the cross and he will recover strength.'[84] When we have exercised ourselves in self-knowledge and reflected upon our sins, if we still feel discouraged or sad, it is important to make sure we also exercise ourselves in another knowledge which will encourage and cheer us. Fr Avila advises that for this purpose there is no knowledge like reflecting on the Lord's Passion.[85] It 'is a book in which [one] can read of the immensity of divine goodness and the gentleness of his love',[86] a love which is ineffable and beyond compare. The 'reason why so many do not serve God is that they do not understand how much God loves them. They do not know what He did for them; that He gave His son for them; that He wept so that they might have happiness and contentment.'[87]

Jesus was most determined when He mounted the cross that He would 'suffer all that would be necessary for our healing;' such was the love which burned within His heart.[88] Our Saint exclaims, 'Such love should surely be enough to make us run in earnest to God, this love should be enough to captivate our hearts forever.'[89] Moreover, if we 'dig deeper with the light of heaven and search into this reliquary of God, full of ineffable secrets, [we] will see within it effects of love that will lead us to wonder more than at what happened exteriorly.'[90] For 'without doubt He loved much more than He suffered, and there remained far greater love [hidden] in His Heart than that which he showed outwardly in His wounds.'[91] His love far 'surpassed all that he suffered exteriorly –although that was ineffable –as the heaven surpasses the earth.'[92]

Whenever we meditate on Christ's Passion, Fr Avila advises that we ask the 'Lord to send the light of the Holy Spirit' so that we can feel with love and compassion that which Christ so lovingly and willing suffered for us. He advises that we place within our heart one of the events which we want to consider, and think about it as if we were present. 'Above all, with a quiet and simple gaze, we should contemplate His most sacred heart.'[93] As we discover God's infinite love for us, there are also many other benefits which we can derive when we meditate on Christ's Passion. We can discover how beautiful and precious grace is and how hideous and harmful sin is.[94] When we come to know God's great love for us, it can make us want to imitate the Lord.[95] By imitating His virtues of patience and humility and His 'loving and compassionate heart, from which everything else proceeds,'[96] we become more and more conformed to Christ. Fr Avila says there is 'no book as effective as the Passion of the Son of God for teaching every kind of virtue and how much sin must be abhorred and virtue loved.'[97] By the favours which Christ did for us on the Cross He truly wishes the fire of His 'love to burn in us so that it sets us aflame, burns us up, and consumes what we are, transforming us into [Him].'[98]

Notes

1   John of Avila, *Audi, Filia—Listen, O Daughter,* translated and introduced by Joan Frances Gormley (New York: Paulist Press, 2006), ch. 5, p. 50. (Hereafter cited as *AF.*)

2   John of Avila, *The Holy Ghost,* translated by Ena Dargan (Dublin: Scepter Limited, 1959), VI, p. 131. (Hereafter cited as *HG.*)

3   *HG,* VI, p. 128.

4   *AF,* ch. 63, p. 188.

5   *AF,* ch. 61, pp. 183–184.

6   *Ibid.,* p. 184.

7   John of Avila, *Letters of Blessed John of Avila,* translated and selected from the Spanish by the Benedictines of Stanbrook (London: Burns & Oates Ltd., 1904), XXII, p. 142. (Hereafter cited as *Letters.*)

8   *AF,* ch. 9, p. 59.

9   *Ibid.*

10 E. Allison Peers, *The Mystics of Spain* (New York: Dover Publications Inc., 2002), p. 72.

11 *Letters,* XIII , pp. 91–92.

12 *HG,* V, p. 108.

13 *HG,* V, p. 119.

14 *AF,* ch. 4, pp. 48–49.

15 *AF,* ch. 3, p. 45.

16 *AF,* ch. 4, p. 47.

17 *Ibid.*

18 *Ibid.,* p. 46.

19 *AF,* ch. 4, p. 47.

20 *HG,* V, p. 113.

21 *Ibid.*

22 *Letters,* XX, pp. 132–133.

23 *Ibid.,* pp. 133–134, *AF,* ch. 4, pp. 46–47.

24 Longaro degli Oddi, *Life of the Blessed Master John of Avila; Secular Priest, Called the Apostle of Andulusia* (London: Burns and Oates, 1898), p. 77.

25 *AF,* ch. 63, p. 190.

26   *Letters,* XIX, p. 121.

27   *AF,* ch. 63, p. 189.

28   *Ibid.*

29   *AF,* ch. 58, p. 179.

30   *AF,* ch. 63, p. 190.

31   *AF,* ch. 21, p. 86.

32   *AF,* ch. 58, p. 179.

33   John of Avila, *Certain Selected Spiritual Epistles* (Rouen: John Le Costurier, 1631), 36, p. 285. (Hereafter cited as *Epistles.*)

34   *AF,* ch. 17, p. 79 .

35   *AF,* ch. 12, p. 66.

36   *Epistles,* 54, pp. 422–423.

37   *AF,* ch. 17, p. 75.

38   *Epistles,* 55, pp. 422–423.

39   *Ibid.,* pp. 424–425.

40   *Epistles,* 55, pp. 424–425.

41   *AF,* ch. 17, p. 75 .

42   *Epistles,* 54, pp. 422–423.

43   *AF,* ch. 17, pp. 75–76.

44   *AF,* ch. 62, p. 187.

45   *Letters,* XXIII, pp. 151–152.

46   *Epistles,* 36, p. 285.

47   *AF,* ch. 67, p. 197.

48   *Letters,* XXIII, pp. 148–149.

49   *AF,* ch. 64, p. 190.

50   *AF,* ch. 59, p. 181.

51   *Ibid.*

52   *AF,* ch. 61, p. 185.

53   *AF,* ch. 77, p. 223.

54   *Letters,* XIX, p. 122.

55   *Epistles,* 56, p. 430.

56   *AF,* ch. 67, p. 197.

57   *Epistles,* 44, pp. 339–340.

58   *Ibid.,* p. 339.

59   *AF,* ch. 23, pp. 90–91.

60   *Letters,* XIV, p. 97.

61   *AF,* ch. 20, p. 84.

62   *Epistles,* 44, p. 335.

63   *Letters,* XVII, p. 107.

64   *Epistles,* 44, pp. 339–340.

65   *Epistles,* 47, p. 367.

66   *Ibid.*

67   *Epistles,* 45, p. 345.

68   *AF,* ch. 20, p. 83.

69   *Epistles,* 47, p. 367.

70   *Ibid.,* pp. 366–367.

71   *Letters,* XVII, p. 106.

72   *AF,* ch. 67, p. 197.

73   *AF,* ch. 18, p. 80.

74   *Letters,* XVII, p. 106.

75   *AF,* ch. 22, p. 89.

76   *AF,* ch. 18, p. 79, *AF,* ch. 23, p. 89.

77   *Epistles,* 27, pp. 225–226.

78   *AF,* ch. 18, p. 79.

79   *AF,* ch. 21, p. 85.

80   *Epistles,* 30, p. 248.

81   *AF,* ch. 47, p. 149.

82   *Ibid.,* p. 150.

83   *Letters,* XXIII, pp. 156–157.

84   *AF,* ch. 68, p. 199.

85   *Ibid.*

86   *AF,* ch. 81, p. 234.

87   *HG,* V, p. 112.

88   *AF,* ch. 69, p. 203.

89   *AF,* ch. 79, p. 229.

90   *Ibid.*

91   John of Avila, 'Treatise on the Love of God' in Luis de la Palma, *The History of the Sacred Passion,* translation revised and edited by Henry James Coleridge (London: Burns and Oates, 1875), p. 148.

92   *AF,* ch. 74, p. 215.

93   *Ibid.,* pp. 214–215.

94   *AF,* ch. 81, p. 234.

95   *AF,* ch. 76, p. 219.

96   *AF,* ch. 81, p. 234.

97   *AF,* ch. 68, p. 199.

98   *AF,* ch. 69, p. 203.

6

JOURNEYING TOWARDS GOD

ADVANCING TOWARDS UNION with God is a beautiful adventure, and certainly never boring. Our whole life is a journey that can be so much greater if we invite the living God into our hearts; for there is no better travel than advancing towards God with a heart inflamed with love. This journey is full of beauty, and the treasure that waits for us at the end is beyond compare. The road, however, is often bumpy. With the strength of the Lord and a heart that is conformed to God's will, we can overcome all the difficulties of life and advance on the path towards union with God. If we truly desire to advance in the spiritual life, we will have to detach ourselves from all that hinders this union. In order to live this Christian life well, we must give our whole heart to God and love Him above all things. We must be determined to live the message of the Gospel so that we can be fully disposed to be open to God's grace. We should not be attached to worldly things or have unhealthy attachments to anything, for this hinders our union with God.[1] This does not mean that we cannot enjoy the gifts that God gives us—like the beauty of creation or time spent with a close friend—God wants us to be happy and gives us things to enjoy. The problem is that we too easily become attached to created things and seek fulfilment in the things themselves rather than in God. Fr Avila says when we 'desire good things, as our own last end, and for love of ourselves, we make ourselves ill; since we invert that order, which the love of God prescribes; which is, to love that, which is good, and ourselves with all, for the service of God'.[2]

On the other hand, when our desires are truly ordered we seek God first and foremost and we are free from inordinate desires which hinder perfect union with God. However, before we reach this stage, we will have to go through certain purifications so that we can be free from attachments which prevent us from progressing in the spiritual life.

> A disciplined human body is an excellent instrument for sanctification, but in the present state of fallen nature it is badly inclined and has an almost irresistible tendency to anything that can give pleasure to the senses. If it is not subjected, it becomes indomitable, and its demands become more and more excessive until it constitutes an obstacle which is incompatible with the spiritual perfection of the soul. St Paul speaks of the necessity of mortifying the body in order to be liberated from its tyranny and to assure one's own salvation: 'I chastise my body and bring it in subjection, lest perhaps after preaching to others, I myself should be rejected.' (1 Co. 9:27)[3]

If a soul is not following God and desires to seek inordinate pleasures, it subordinates its reason to its passions.[4] The soul that is living a morally good life will be more ordered; nevertheless, the passions may need to be stilled so that the soul can experience the fullness of God, for it will not enjoy the freedom from self-love that is needed to be intimately united with God.[5] If we put ourselves in the hands of Jesus, the divine physician, He will give us the healing we need. The Holy Spirit will burn away all that is not holy, for 'this Teacher and Paraclete performs spiritual cures among those souls in whom He dwells and with whom He is in union through grace.'[6] He moulds us and sets us free from that which keeps us bound.[7] He purifies us and removes from us all things that are displeasing to God, and fosters revives and increases within us all things that are agreeable to God. He brings transformation and changes the human heart. He strengthens and consoles the soul in which He dwells.[8] 'So powerful is the fire of the Holy Spirit ... it remains ever alight; it fills and inflames our hearts, burning away all evil.'[9] There is 'no power on earth that can accomplish as much.' Only the Holy Spirit can transform hearts, even the most hardened.[10] He opens our 'sense to the things of God' and subjects our 'affections to reason.' What was sweet to us he makes bitter and what we before found tasteless we now desire.[11] There are many people who have been so changed by the power of the Holy Spirit that it is plain to see their change was not accomplished by human strength, but is indeed a great grace which happened by the power of the Holy Spirit.[12]

As a result of this healing purification, our senses become much more docile and subject to reason. The soul that has been purified gains a healthy detachment from creatures; it is not attached to temporal things and can therefore use them wisely and profitably, without being attached to them or having a love which rests in them.[13] Consequently we will have 'well-ordered affections of the soul.'[14] The fact that we must go through this purification, which at times can be very difficult, should not make us sad or discouraged; for the person that allows God to mould and purify his or her heart will not be disappointed. Before the soul was purified it was prevented from receiving the fullness of God's light and still did not have the purity that is needed to be intimately united with God.[15] The 'more a soul is free of passions and is purged from affections for earthly things, the higher it rises in the contemplation of truth and tastes how sweet the Lord is.'[16] It will have a 'sweet and delightful life of love with God.'[17] Furthermore, it will be at peace because peace comes as a consequence of a person being ordered within[18] and having an intimate relationship with God.

The Means of Purification

A simple way to understand *detachment* can be taken from St Teresa of Avila, who describes it as 'not paying attention to what doesn't bring us closer to God.'[19] Of course this is easier said than done; nevertheless, there are various ways in which we can help ourselves to become detached. For example we can try to lessen excessive amusements or idle chatting; we can use our time wisely by praying more and doing works that are for the good of our neighbour;[20] we can be moderate with the things in which we tend to over-indulge. In order to be so completely detached that we can receive the fullness of God, we need God's help; for without it we will never be able to attain a high degree of perfection.

One of the ways God helps us to grow in holiness is to allow us to undergo certain trials. This purification can be painful, and many people will want to turn back and abandon the path that leads to holiness. When souls are faced with various trials they think that if they follow the easier path—the wider road which leads to destruction—they will have more peace than when they follow the 'narrow way of virtue that leads to life.'[21] However, there is no other road by which one can reach Christian perfection and union with God, and there is no lasting happiness apart from union with God in Christ. God wants to heal us and make us whole. It is inevitable that we will have to pass through trials, but the Lord always rescues us and brings us through these trials restored and purged from unruly passions.[22] We should not become discouraged when we undergo trials; rather we should, as Fr Avila advises, learn how to draw profit from all our sorrows, because they 'bring great riches to the soul' (Ws 3).[23] Master Avila encourages us not to turn back from the narrow path: 'Let this cross be dear to you, it is heavy indeed, but remember that the cross is the ladder to paradise.'[24] Our Saint goes on, 'Let none deceive themselves, but let them feel assured that, as the King of heaven entered His kingdom through tribulations, we must reach it by the same path. There is but one way—"Christ, and Christ crucified!"'[25]

Fr Avila's words seem very strong, but he is clear in pointing out that imitation of Christ is the only way to reach holiness. He does not hide the hard sayings of the Gospel. He adheres to the words that Jesus Himself speaks in the Gospel of Mathew 7:13, the teaching of the narrow way. Our Saint remarks 'Did you think perhaps, that it was some dainty and delightful thing, to serve Christ our Lord? Or that you undertook some trifling business, when you began to place your love on him? They who fight the battles of love must die daily, as S. Paul did.'[26] Christ is our model and guide, and if we are to be disciples of Christ, we must take up our cross and follow Him. This takes courage, but if we follow the Lord with our whole heart and remain faithful to the Gospel message by living a good moral life, we will have the courage needed to advance on the road to holiness. However, those who are careless in the service of God and suffer from mediocrity will never 'posses that vigor of heart and courage that follow from a good and diligent life'.[27] A courageous heart is the fruit of living a good life and 'those who live well find [it] within themselves without searching.'[28] We should pray that God will give us the means to remain strong in faith and love under trials, and we will gain even greater strength and courage. As Fr Avila explains:

> A large fire is increased, rather than quenched by the wind, so, though a weak love of God is, like a candle, easily extinguished by the first puff of air, yet true charity gains force and courage by its trials. This is the fire which comes down from heaven which no water of tribulation can extinguish.[29]

Interior Trials — When God Hides His Face

The trials that a person can go through in life are numerous, and they can all help to purify a person's soul. There are some particular trials however that the Lord will often send to His beloved friends, to souls who have already advanced considerably in the spiritual life. These trials wound a person in spirit, for trials of a more temporal nature do not have much effect on these people since they live by the spirit and are already detached from temporal things.[30] These trials are all part of the purification a soul needs in order to advance further in the spiritual life. God is like a wise physician. He knows exactly what a soul needs at each moment. Sometimes He gives favours, lights, and consolations; at other times, He hides Himself. When God hides His face, it seems to the soul that He is nowhere to be found. In Catholic Tradition, this has been called by different names—Fr Avila calls this a trial of faith,[31] while St John of the Cross refers to it as 'the dark night'.[32] When God hides His face and does not answer when we call, it can cause great interior suffering and we are tried in our 'confidence, love and patience.'[33]

Interior suffering can be a lot more difficult than trials which are of a more exterior nature. The outward trials which Jesus endured on the cross were great indeed, but this could not be compared to the suffering that went unseen; therefore when we suffer interior trials we become much more conformed to Christ.[34] The anguish caused within the soul during these trials is intense, for it finds nowhere to rest; nothing but God can comfort it for it is God Who has hidden Himself. The soul goes through a mighty desert and darkness, and must seek the Lord until He finally delivers it from this trial.[35] The torment from one of these trials can redound even to the body itself. In this case the whole person, both interior and exterior, has the discomfort of the cross laid upon him or her. This causes a person so much suffering that he or she will beseech the Lord's help; yet the Lord appears to be as deaf, and more hidden than ever from the soul, even more than if there were many walls between them. The soul feels that God has abandoned it and that He is showing it disfavour.[36]

Fr Avila likens this kind of interior trial to a martyrdom. He explains that there have been many martyrs who have won glorious crowns for themselves at the hands of terrible executioners. However, there is another type of martyrdom, which is interior and invisible; these kinds are martyrdoms, says Fr Avila, are 'as great, or greater' than bloody martyrdom. In the case of bloody martyrdom, a person is tormented at the hands of another human being, and God sends comfort, so that the torments are more tolerable. However, when the Lord sends interior trials by hiding Himself from the soul, the devils try through many evil devices to torment a person's mind, which is much more sensitive than the body.[37] As Fr Avila explains, the poor soul, instead of going through a bloody martyrdom at the hand of executioners, suffers at the hands of the demons. These demons are more vicious and cruel than any human executioner, especially since they torment people much 'more in the soul, than in the body.' The soul that undergoes such trials truly suffers a type of 'martyrdom for love of Christ' and is martyred for the Lord's service.[38] Our Saint however, points out that even though God hides Himself from us for a time, He is still very close for our defence. For if the Lord had not been near us our enemies would have swallowed us up ten thousand times over, (Ps 124).[39]

The soul who experiences this kind of darkness has not been abandoned by God; He is very close. If we experience this kind of darkness, we should take up the *shield of Faith* and cast off all dismay, believing that we are loved by God, for these trials are sent to strengthen our trust in Him.[40] God is hiding Himself, but watches to see what we will do when He no longer blesses us with His intimate embrace. He watches like a 'jealous Spouse' desiring that we will remain confident in Him.[41] When God seems to have forgotten us we should place our confidence in Him all the more, for God wants us to trust in Him not only when we feel He is close and giving us comfort, but even when He has hidden His face from us.[42] The Lord has hidden Himself for a time to try our faith, but He is very close and always defends those who call upon Him, and He delivers them from all their troubles.[43] Therefore, we should seek the Lord even when it feels like He is absent, or sleeping, and persist in seeking Him until we have woken Him and until He tells us that we have been 'faithful in his absence.'[44]

These trials can cause a lot of distress, and we may even begin to wonder how we stand in the sight of God. Our Saint explains that there few things in the world by which we can be so effectively purged from sin and taught so many truths as when we experience these inward struggles of darkness and obscurity.[45] The person who humbles himself or herself and loves God as steadfastly and sincerely as possible in the midst of such trials is making a great act of faith and love.[46] For a soul shows true faith when it believes even though no signs are given, and not just without signs 'but even against them.'[47] Having remained faithful, it then enters into the most intimate and secret heart of the Lord.[48]

The Benefits received from Suffering Trials

Apart from the trials which God sends to more advanced souls, there are many hardships which the trials of life bring. In Fr Avila's letters, he is always encouraging his directees to embrace their trials with love. Souls who understand the benefits that can be gained will make good use of these hardships.[49] We take on many difficulties just to gain temporal things; how much greater are the treasures which await the person who endures hardship for the sake of the kingdom! Our Saint comments that if worldly people were told they could gain great happiness by walking a very long way, it is certain they would have no problem undertaking such a long journey. Furthermore, if they were told that they could gain a 'whole kingdom,' and if they continued, on this walk with the same pace, they would never be deprived of this reward, then what worldly person would not be a great walker? In fact, he or she would probably never be persuaded to keep still. If visible and temporal things can have such an effect, what will the love of that which is eternal and invisible work in our souls! If we know about the benefits, we will take great care to follow the way of the Lord with a strong and lively resolution, an even stronger resolution than the one we had when we first started.[50] This strength and persistence is needed to advance in the spiritual life, and not grow weary on the road that leads to perfection.

The benefits which come as a result of enduring patiently with hardships are many. First of all they cleanse our soul from sins committed in the past, purifying the heart like fire purifies gold.[51] They can also make us draw much closer to God, for when we suffer, the pain is much more likely to make us seek the Lord than if we were prospering. When we are struggling, we may become impatient and fall into sin, but the likelihood of us falling into sin when we are prospering is much greater.[52] Through troubles and temptations we will also be 'animated to serve God better,' since we see how much we need Him.[53] Hardships make us seek God, they help to keep us humble, and foster the development of patience. Patience in turn strengthens the faith, hope and love which we have in Christ.[54] The benefits of such suffering are so great that St Paul calls us to 'rejoice in our sufferings, knowing that suffering produces endurance, and endurance produces character, and character produces hope, and hope does not disappoint us, because God's love has been poured into our hearts through the Holy Spirit who has been given to us' (Rm 5:3–5). If we diligently follow the path of virtue, we will be freed from many dangers and receive an abundance of blessings.[55] The Lord allows us to undergo certain trials for our own good — to help us grow in virtue — for there cannot be true virtue unless it has been tried and tested.[56] Growth in virtue is promoted through trials.[57] In His love and mercy God allows us to undergo such trials in order to gain a crown; He does this in the measure that we can handle, not so little that we cannot gain treasure for our crown, and not so much that it will surpass our weakness.[58]

Bearing with trials can be very wearisome and often requires courage, but Fr Avila explains that it is very important that friends of God are prepared to undergo trials, because without trials our virtues will be 'like an unwalled city, which falls at the first onslaught.'[59] There are many of God's friends who have been greatly helped and enriched through trials and struggles.[60] The communications that St Paul received from God were so abundant that if God had not permitted him to be tried through troubles, discomforts, and a bad angel to beat him, he may have become prideful. However, through interior and exterior suffering his soul was kept secure and he was happy to suffer for the glory of God.[61] When things cause bitterness and this is endured for love of the Lord alone, a person is 'more secure from [self] interest or complacence.'[62]

There are some people, that become very proud when they receive any small favour from God.[63] In fact, there are very few people who can enjoy God's sweet delights without some admixture of pride or inordinate clinging to such favours.[64] Some people's hearts are so hard that unless they are constantly spurred on by divine consolations, they do not walk in the ways of God. Such people need to undergo many hardships in order to remain humble. God allows them to go through trials and temptations, and sometimes even to fall into sin, so that they become more humble. In fact, He often allows such people to be so tried, that in their utter desperation to rid themselves of their miseries, they humbly seek remedy from the Lord.[65]

According to Fr Avila 'prosperity is much more to be feared than adversity', for in prosperity there is more chance that a person will turn away from God.[66] If the Lord is not consoling us with sweetness and delights, it is not a bad place to be. The Lord keeps us in a safe place through trials and tribulation, for these trials will benefit us for all eternity. If the Lord sends spiritual consolations, there is profit, but sometimes the profit gained is not as much as the delight that was enjoyed.[67] On the last day God will not ask us how many comforts and delights we have enjoyed, but what struggles we have undergone without failing in faith or love.[68] There is no price that is too great to gain eternal life—it is a true gem of inestimable value.[69] Fr Avila remarks, 'Remember, that we shall soon quit this world, and then all the past will seem to us like a short dream, and we shall see that it is better to have labored than to have rested here.'[70]

The spiritual journey is not always easy but the reward that awaits us in heaven is beyond compare, and the peace and joy we can have in this life far outweigh the difficulties. Therefore, in the midst of trials, instead of focusing on how difficult the trial looks on the surface, Fr Avila recommends that we should try to focus on 'the hidden gift that God sends underneath it'.[71] Life is like a tapestry; the back of the tapestry looks very messy, but when the tapestry is turned over we see the beautiful picture which has been woven on the other side. God weaves the different situations of our life together; it often looks messy, but the skilful hand of God weaves all the trials and struggles of life and uses them as colours to enhance the beautiful big picture.

We may have to suffer for a time, but we should look to God, trusting that He will work all things for our good (Rm 8:28). We can be assured that when we go through trials He will always give us the grace and strength we need. Our Saint explains that God does not take pleasure in the things people have to suffer, for He is a God of infinite mercy.[72] If the Lord chastises, He does it for our good.[73] If He has to reprove, He will also console those He admonishes; this is why the Holy Spirit is called the Comforter.[74] Our Saint explains that often God will give us some kind of consolation even before we undergo various trials in order to help us endure in the future.[75] He also says that God cannot help but comfort His afflicted friends, when He sees this is best for them.[76]

If God sometimes seems not to grant all that we desire, it is to give us something which is better for us; according to Fr Avila,

> This is how the heavenly Physician treats the
> sick who go to Him wishing to be cured, rather
> than to taste pleasant medicines. Do not with-

draw yourself from His hands however painful
His remedies may be. Ask Him not to do your
will in what He does, but to do His own.[77]

The divine physician will always give us the grace and
strength for all that we must endure. To one of his
directees who was undergoing various trials, Fr Avila
writes, 'He hath given that which he knew to be best
for you; and if you think it heavy consider that he who
sends it, will give you shoulders wherewith to bear
it.'[78] Souls who instead of becoming weary and anxious, accept their suffering for love of God, find
strength, comfort and support from God, for He is very
near them; He fills them with His love and treats them
as most beloved.[79] Love can make us embrace all
hardships and help us overcome them all 'by the
burning charity that God has kindled' in our hearts.[80]
'So powerful is the fire of the Holy Spirit, that it
mounts upwards, and gives us a love and trust in God
that no water of sorrow or affliction can extinguish.'[81]

Trials and Temptations—The Battle

If we are serious about following Christ, some of the
trials and temptations which we will have to face on
our spiritual journey will be attacks from the evil one.
We cannot advance on the road towards holiness
without various struggles. Fr Avila says, 'Be certain
that the way of perfect virtue is an exceedingly bitter
battle against very strong enemies within and outside
us.'[82] When a person really turns from love of the
world and starts to strive for perfection, the demons
start to stir up wars against the soul.[83] As St Paul
reminds us, 'Our struggle is not against enemies of
flesh and blood, but against the rulers, against the
authorities, against the cosmic powers of this present

darkness, against the spiritual forces of evil in the heavenly places' (Ep 6:12). They will be up to all different kinds of tricks, and if they do not win one battle with us, they will try different strategies, thinking they can overcome in some other way. 'The demons envy our well-being so much that they try all sorts of ways to keep us from enjoying what they have lost.'[84] St Peter reminds us, 'Be sober and vigilant. Your opponent the devil is prowling around like a roaring lion looking for someone to devour. Resist him, steadfast in faith,' (1P 5:8-9). Fr Avila explains that when the devil sees he cannot overcome us by his cunning, which he did as a 'hidden dragon,' he then become like a 'ferocious lion' (cf. 1P 5:8). He will try to inspire fear in us 'by his roaring'; when this happens we must have recourse to the Lord and watch and pray with diligence.[85]

Unless the Lord allows it, the devil does not have any power and can do nothing. Furthermore, God never allows the enemy to afflict us unless it is for our greater good and for the utter confusion of the enemy. Fr Avila reminds us that

> This is in accord with the Scripture that 'God will deride those who deride and that the one who dwells in heaven will mock them' (Ps 2:4). For although this dragon plays and mocks in the sea of this world, tempting and striking the servants of God, God mocks him (Ps 37:13) by drawing good from the devil's wicked deeds. When the devil thinks that he is doing most harm to the virtuous, he benefits them most.[86]

The enemy, seeing that the soul benefits so much from all of the wicked deeds he began, becomes so ashamed and confounded, that he wishes that he had never started playing such wicked games—because the soul that he was trying to harm has benefited so much. 'The wickedness and the snare that he stretched out for others fell upon his own head (cf. Ps 35:8). He ends up dead with envy, seeing those whom he tempted go free, singing with joy: "The snare has been broken and we are free; our help is the Lord who made heaven and earth"(Ps 124:7–8).'[87]

It is no surprise that the enemy torments the person who desires to serve Christ. These torments are trials of faith and love which the Lord allows his children to endure.[88] If we decided to yield to sin, we would soon see that the persecution would cease. However, by allowing us to undergo trials God gives us the opportunity to grow in virtue and advance in the spiritual life.[89] There is beautiful treasure to be gained by resisting the devil and trusting in the Lord. All the troubles and temptations a soul has endured are tempered when it sees the benefit it has gained.[90] Instead of receiving chains with which the enemy wanted to bind it, the soul receives a crown of blessings.[91]

Fr Avila advises us to have courage, trust in the Lord, and not grow weary of gaining new stones for our crown; for even though the enemy throws stones that can hurt for a little while, afterwards they become precious stones which we have gained all for ourselves.[92] Having been tried we emerge with many blessings. We should therefore, thank the Lord Who is all good and all powerful, and Who would 'never permit any evil except to bring good from it by a higher means. Nor would He permit our enemy and those who belong to him to afflict us, unless it is for the great confusion of the enemy and for the good of the one afflicted.'[93]

Take Up the Shield of Faith

We must be strong in the battle against the enemy, for our Saint says, 'There is nothing more harmful for one entering this war than to take along pusillanimity of heart. Whoever has this will flee even from shadows.'[94] The desert Fathers experienced so many spiritual battles that they understood just how necessary it is for people to have a courageous heart.[95] The principal aim of the enemy—in the battles he wages—is to take away a person's courage so that the good which has already been started will be abandoned. He tries to disturb prayer with turmoil and sometimes tries to hinder sleep.[96] The demons never get tired; they can be around us at any time of the day or night.[97] Sometimes, the enemy causes so much fear that the person trembles in anguish.[98]

St Peter and St Paul teach us that the key to overcoming the attacks of the enemy is *Faith*. Fr Avila explains:

> This is because, when a soul, by the love of God that is the life of faith, despises the prosperity and adversity of the world, and believes and trusts in God, whom it does not see, there is no way by which the demon may enter.[99]

We should therefore, 'take up the shield of faith with which [we] may be able to extinguish all the darts burning with fire.'(Ep 6:10–11, 16). According to Fr Avila, St Antony of the Desert—the 'great conqueror of demons'—said that 'against the demons, the sign of the cross and faith, sometimes meaning confidence, are for us an impregnable wall.'[100] We should trust in God's mercy when faced with all kinds of dangers, for we may find that we gain a lot of courage to fight the spiritual battle we face—a courage which is indeed necessary for such a war.[101] We must therefore try to remain firm in faith amongst the waves of trial, even when it seems that we are sinking. The Lord wants us to be extremely courageous; when the Apostles were in the boat with Jesus they became afraid because the waves were crashing all around them, but Jesus woke up and said 'Why fear you, o men of little faith?'[102]

When we are faced with all kinds of trials from the enemy, Fr Avila advises us to use the means which the Church provides to strengthen us. 'Since, this enemy is more powerful than we are, we ought to take advantage of the supernatural "shield of faith," shielding ourselves with something from our faith such as with a word of God, the reception of the sacraments, or a doctrine of the church.'[103] Since this war is one of trickery and 'proceeds by way of fear,' we must take courage and have a firm hope in the Lord and invoke Him at all times.[104] We must see to it that we do not let ourselves be overcome by sadness and try our best to be cheerful. We must learn to stand strong in the face of trial and tribulation, for we can overcome every trial if we arm ourselves with faith and love.[105] We should say to ourselves that the Lord takes care of those who love Him; what can harm us? We aspire to no other joy, other than the joy of the Lord, whatever the cost. When the devil finds a soul so courageous and so fully armed, he will not be able to drag it down; on the contrary, he will be afraid to assault such a soul.[106]

On our own, we are weak and fragile; but if we have recourse to the Lord and hide under His loving protection, we can overcome all things. In fact, Fr Avila says that it is possible we 'will gain more merit in a single year than … in ten.'[107] The Lord wants us to have total confidence in Him. Fr Avila has no doubt that those who give their whole selves to God will see what true a friend the Lord 'is to those in tribulation; how He dwells with them and provides for them.'[108] When we undergo trials, Fr Avila encourages us to raise our eyes to heaven and commend ourselves to the Lord. We should offer everything to Him and undergo our struggles for love of Him; then our burden will become light and we will receive great reward.[109]

True Love for the Lord

As we continue to grow in the spiritual life, our love for God also continues to grow. We can become so inflamed with this love that we will do anything in His service. On the other hand, a person may think he or she has a deep love for God, but this love is far from perfect. God is much more concerned about the motive of a person's actions, rather than the number or greatness of the acts. Works performed with more love are far more pleasing to God, and a small sacrifice done with great love is much better than the greatest austerities performed with little or no love.[110] Fr Avila warns us that we should not be tricked into thinking that if charity is not accompanied by feelings of joy, it is worthless. He explains that the enemy is well aware that we can be tricked into thinking this way; therefore, this enemy is always trying to make people feel dry and lukewarm, so that they will eventually give up on their holy works. True charity is not based on feeling; rather, it is an act of the will.[111] According to Fr Avila, one thing that proves our love is if we stand for God's honour in times of temptation. God rejoices when His friends remain faithful in times of tribulation, for He wants His friends to be faithful and patient under trials.[112] If we are receiving revelations, comforts, or delights from the hand of God, it is much harder to know whether we truly love God or whether we love the things that we are receiving more than we love the giver of these gifts. However, we have grounds to believe that we truly love God when our hardships are born out of love for Him.[113]

The Summit of Love

As souls advance in the spiritual life, they become more and more aware of the treasure of the Cross—a treasure which can purify not only their own souls but one which can also help win many souls for Jesus. The love of holy souls can grow so strong that not only do they desire to follow God's will and accept all hardships of life with love, but they even find sweetness in suffering. It is important to understand that without the grace of the Holy Spirit, sweetness in suffering would be impossible. It is the Holy Spirit Who begins to remove the 'veil that hides from human eyes the holy, the unutterable and divine revelation of the cross.'[114] Through the gift of wisdom—one of the seven gifts of the Holy Spirit received in the Sacrament of Baptism—as the soul advances toward union with God, it can begin to see and judge things from a divine point of view rather than a human point of view. The person will see what the limited human intellect cannot understand and look on suffering in a different light. The Holy Spirit gives His beloved souls a profound penetration into the mystery of suffering so that they see the true and immense value of the Cross.

There are souls who know of this love because God has revealed to them His 'secrets and has given them to understand these mysteries.'[115]

Notes

1   John of the Cross, *Ascent of Mount Carmel* in *Collected Works*, translated by Kieran Kavanaugh and Otilio Rodriguez (Washington, D.C.: ICS Publications, 1991), Bk I, ch. 6, p. 84.

2   John of Avila, *Certain Selected Spiritual Epistles* (Rouen: John Le Costurier, 1631), 31, p. 250. (Hereafter cited as *Epistles*.)

3   Antonio Royo, and Jordan Aumann, *The Theology of Christian Perfection* (Dubuque, IA: The Priory Press, 1962), p. 284.

4   John of Avila, *Letters of Blessed John of Avila*, translated and selected from the Spanish by the Benedictines of Stanbrook (London: Burns & Oates Ltd., 1904), V, p. 51. (Hereafter cited as *Letters*.)

5   John of Avila, *Audi, Filia—Listen, O Daughter*, translated and introduced by Joan Frances Gormley (New York: Paulist Press, 2006), ch. 77, pp. 224–225. (Hereafter cited as *AF*.)

6   John of Avila, *The Holy Ghost*, translated by Ena Dargan (Dublin: Scepter Limited, 1959), IV, p. 92. (Hereafter cited as *HG*.)

7   *Letters*, XXIV, p. 160.

8   *HG*, III, p. 71.

9   *Letters*, XXIV, p. 160.

10 *HG*, III, p. 71.

11 *AF*, ch. 66, p. 195.

12 *HG*, III, p. 72.

13 *AF*, ch. 4, p. 47.

14 *ST*, I-II, q. 69, a. 2, ad 3.

15 *AF*, ch. 77, pp. 224–225.

16 Thomas Aquinas, *Commentary on the Gospel of St. John*, Part I: Chapters 1–7, translated by James A. Weisheipl (Albany, NY: Magi Books, Inc., 1998), ch. 1, lec. 11, n. 213. http://dhspriory.org/thomas/SSJohn.htm, accessed May 21, 2012.

17 John of the Cross, *Dark Night of the Soul* in *The Collected Works*,

translated by Kieran Kavanaugh and Otilio Rodriguez (Washington, D.C.: ICS Publications, 1991), Bk.I, Prologue, p. 360.

[18] Thomas Aquinas, *Commentary on the Gospel of St John*, Part II: Chapters 8–21, translated by Fabian R. Larcher (Albany, NY: Magi Books, Inc., 1998), ch. 14, lec. 7, n. 1962. http://dhspriory.org/thomas/SSJohn.htm, accessed May 21, 2012.

[19] Teresa of Avila, *The Book of Her Life* in *The Collected Works*, vol. I, translated by Kieran Kavanaugh and Otilio Rodriguez (Washington, D.C.: ICS Publications, 1980), ch. 40, p. 278, as quoted in Thomas Dubay, *Fire Within* (San Francisco: Ignatius Press, 1989), p. 150.

[20] Thomas Dubay, *Fire Within* (San Francisco: Ignatius Press, 1989), p. 151.

[21] *AF*, ch. 27, p. 100.

[22] *Epistles*, 51, pp. 394–395.

[23] *Letters*, XX, p. 124.

[24] Longaro degli Oddi, *Life of the Blessed Master John of Avila; Secular Priest, Called the Apostle of Andulusia* (London: Burns and Oates, 1898), p. 49.

[25] *Letters*, V, pp. 50–51.

[26] *Epistles*, 44, pp. 333–334.

[27] *AF*, ch. 23, p. 92.

[28] *Ibid.*, p. 93.

[29] *Letters*, VI, pp. 56–57.

[30] *Epistles*, 51, p. 388.

[31] *Epistles*, 43, p. 323.

[32] John of the Cross, *Dark Night*, Bk. II.

[33] *AF*, ch. 30, p. 108.

[34] *Epistles*, 42, p. 320.

[35] *Epistles*, 44, p. 333.

[36] *Ibid.*, p. 332.

[37] *Ibid.*

[38] *Epistles*, 30, p. 247.

[39] *Ibid.*, p. 241.

[40] *Epistles*, 44, p. 338.

[41] *Epistles*, 11, p. 80.

[42] *Epistles*, 52, p. 401.

43   *Epistles,* 30, p. 241 and p. 244.
44   *Epistles,* 52, p. 401.
45   *Epistles,* 51, p. 388.
46   *Epistles,* 44, pp. 336–337.
47   *Ibid.,* p. 334.
48   *Ibid.,* pp. 334–335.
49   *Ibid.*
50   *Epistles,* 25, p. 215.
51   *Letters,* XX, p. 124.
52   *Epistles,* 44, pp. 329–330.
53   *AF,* ch. 15, p. 71.
54   *Epistles,* 41, p. 316.
55   *AF,* ch. 37, p. 123.
56   *Epistles,* 30, p. 244.
57   *Epistles,* 34, p. 272.
58   *Epistles,* 51, p. 391.
59   *Letters,* XIX, p. 123.
60   *AF,* ch. 70, p. 207.
61   *Epistles,* 44, p. 330.
62   *Epistles,* 43, pp. 326–327.
63   *AF,* ch. 24, p. 94.
64   *Epistles,* 43, pp. 325–326.
65   *AF,* ch. 24, p. 94.
66   *Epistles,* 44, pp. 329–330.
67   *Epistles,* 43, pp. 325–326.
68   *Ibid.,* p. 325.
69   *Letters,* V, p. 55.
70   *Letters,* XX, p. 124.
71   *AF,* ch. 26, p. 97.
72   *Letters,* V, p. 52.
73   *HG,* II, p. 31.
74   *HG,* III, p. 69.
75   *AF,* ch. 26, p. 98.
76   *Epistles,* 43, pp. 325–326.
77   *Letters,* V, p. 53.

78   *Epistles,* 32, p. 258.
79   *Epistles,* 41, pp. 315–316.
80   *Letters,* VI, p. 59.
81   *Letters,* XXIV, p. 160.
82   *AF,* ch. 23, p. 91.
83   *Ibid.,* pp. 90–91.
84   *AF,* ch. 29, p. 102.
85   *Ibid.,* pp. 102–103.
86   *AF,* ch. 28, p. 102.
87   *Ibid.*
88   *Epistles,* 30, p. 244.
89   *AF,* ch. 27, p. 100.
90   *Epistles,* 27, p. 226.
91   *AF,* ch. 28, p. 102.
92   *Epistles,* 27, pp. 226–227.
93   *AF,* ch. 28, p. 102.
94   *AF,* ch. 23, p. 91.
95   *AF,* ch. 29, p. 104.
96   *Ibid.,* p. 103.
97   *AF,* ch. 6, p. 53.
98   *AF,* ch. 29, p. 103.
99   *Ibid.*
100 *Ibid.,* p. 104.
101 *Ibid.,* p. 103.
102 *Epistles,* 30, p. 245.
103 *AF,* ch. 30, p. 110–111.
104 *AF,* ch. 29, p. 103.
105 *Epistles,* 45, p. 344.
106 *Epistles,* 27, p. 227.
107 *HG,* III, 69.
108 *Letters,* V, p. 53.
109 *HG,* III, 69.
110 *Letters,* XXII, p. 143–144.
111 *Letters,* XX, p. 133.
112 *AF,* ch. 29, p. 106.

113 *Epistles,* 41, pp. 317–18; *Epistles,* 44, pp. 336–337.
114 Luis M. Martinez, *Sanctifier,* translated by Sister M. Aquinas (Boston: Pauline Books and Media, 1985), p. 108.
115 John of Avila, 'Treatise on the Love of God' in Luis de la Palma, *The History of the Sacred Passion,* translation revised and edited by Henry James Coleridge (London: Burns and Oates, 1875), p. 149.

CONCLUSION

DO YOU LOVE ME?

F WE WANT TO grow in the spiritual life, *love* is the answer; 'for holiness comes from love, and the greater the love, the greater the saint.'[1] In the previous chapters, we have looked at Fr Avila's teaching on the stages of prayer, various experiences we can have at prayer, the importance of self-knowledge and having a healthy detachment from the things of the world, and how to better understand the trials we may face on our spiritual journey. All of this information gives us the advice we need and helps us to discern some of the basic and essential points for advancing in the spiritual life. Fr Avila's advice is for people of all vocations; the substance of his message is applicable in every state of life. Fr Avila never tries to hide the fact that the spiritual journey takes effort and is not always an easy road. We should not become disheartened if we feel overwhelmed by some of his difficult teachings. Growth in the spiritual life takes time, and without a miracle, we will never reach perfection all at once. God is not asking this of us; all He asks for is our love, and that we trust in His mercy. God knows that we are fragile and weak, and that without His help and grace, we can do nothing. We must always remember the mercy of God; for if we believe in God's love, we must believe in His mercy. Bl John Paul II, in his encyclical on the *Mercy of God*, proclaims, 'Believing in this love means *believing in mercy*. For mercy is an indispensable dimension of love; it is as it were love's second name and, at the same time, the specific manner in which love is revealed and effected.'[2]

We should strive to follow the teaching of Fr Avila, but never try to do this relying on our own strength alone. Rather, we should learn to abandon ourselves to the Lord, trusting in His mercy and asking Him to give us the grace and strength to love and follow Him. God is pleased with the soul that recognises its weakness and relies on Him in all the situations of the spiritual life. It is love, trust, and abandonment which move the heart of God and lead a soul to sanctity; God grants mercy and grace to those who trust in Him with the abandonment of a little child. The Saint of love, whom St Pius X called the greatest Saint of modern times, St Therese of Lisieux, exclaims, 'Ah! if all weak and imperfect souls felt what the littlest of all soul feels … not one would despair of reaching the summit of the mountain of love, since Jesus does not ask for great actions but only abandonment and gratitude.'[3] No one should be discouraged, for growth in the spiritual life is not so much about what we can do; rather, it is about recognising our human weakness and our need for the grace of God, and cooperating with the grace which He gives us. As St Paul reminds us, it is in our weakness that He is strong (2 Co 12:7–10). All that God asks is that we have the will to love and follow Him. If we ask Him to help us in all humility, He will always give us His grace. Love, trust, and humility are far more pleasing to God than all the greatest of works which are performed without love. 'The smallest actions done out of love are the ones which charm His Heart.'[4] Jesus 'is content with a glance, a sigh of love;'[5] He desires simply our love. No great works are necessary; for 'without love all works are nothing, even the most dazzling, such as raising the dead to life and converting peoples.'[6] It is our love—not just our works—for which the Lord Jesus waits.

God invites us all into a deep and intimate relationship with Himself. He wants us all to be happy; no one is excluded from love and friendship with Him. He waits to shower us all with His love, and He 'cannot be satisfied, until He has raised to His Sacred Heart even the least of us; and there, like a runaway lamb, at the shepherd's bosom we may rest, held tenderly...'[7] If we open our hearts to God, learning to rely on Him in all things, we will grow in love and friendship with Him. As we spend time with the Lord in prayer, our friendship will continue to develop; for there is no limit to how much we can grow in our relationship with the Lord. If we remain faithful in our friendship with Him, love can become so enkindled within our hearts that it will burn continually and urge us to constantly seek God's holy will and to please Him;[8] for the more a person's love for God increases the more he or she desires to serve God perfectly in 'pure love.'[9]

The key to advancing in the spiritual life is to try and follow the will of God in the small daily tasks of life. Discerning our vocation in life is important—we need to discern whether the Lord is calling us to a priestly vocation, consecrated life, marriage, or the single life. The Lord Jesus assures us that if we truly desire to follow His will and try to remain faithful to the message of the Gospel, He will always lead and guide us, and we will not miss the calling He has for our lives. Jesus promises, 'I am the good shepherd; I know my own and my own know me ... My sheep hear my voice, and I know them, and they follow me,' (Jn 10:14, 27). We are all on a spiritual journey and God has a plan for each and every one of us; each soul is unique and therefore each person's journey will be very different. One thing, however, remains the same for all of us—we are all called to a deep intimate relationship with the Lord, no matter what our vocation. God uses various means to bring people to a deep relationship with Himself, but there is a general path which we must all follow; without this, we cannot advance on the way towards deep union with the Lord.

The Lord of infinite mercy, Who has created each one of us in His image, reminds us, 'Before I formed you in the womb I knew you,' (Jr 1:5). In the fullness of time, this same Lord took on human flesh (cf. Ga 4:4–5) and laid down His life for us (Jn 10:17–18, Ga 1:4). He has called each one of us to a unique vocation and a unique mission. To discern the call of our lives is to hear the voice of the Shepherd and follow wherever He leads. As He did with St Peter on the shore of the Sea of Tiberius 2000 years ago (Jn 21:15–19), Jesus asks each one of us again and again, 'Do you love me?' He beckons us—every day and every hour and every minute of our lives—to answer Him just as St Peter did all those years ago. If we remain faithful in the little things, and if we follow the teaching of the Gospel—if we give our whole mind and heart to Him—we can indeed say, 'Yes Lord, you know that I love you.'

Notes

1   John of Avila, *Letters of Blessed John of Avila*, translated and selected from the Spanish by the Benedictines of Stanbrook (London: Burns & Oates Ltd., 1904), XV, p. 98.

2   Pope John Paul II, *Dives in Misericordia*, 7.

3   Thérèse of Lisieux, *Letters of St Thérèse of Lisieux, General Correspondence*, vol. II, translated from the Original Manuscripts

by John Clarke (Washington, D.C.: ICS Publications, 1988), Lt. 196, p. 994.

4   Thérèse of Lisieux, *General Correspondence* II, Lt. 191, p. 966.

5   *Ibid.*, p. 965.

6   Thérèse of Lisieux, *Story of a Soul*, 3rd edition, translated from the Original Manuscripts by John Clarke (Washington, D.C.: ICS Publications, 1996), p. 175.

7   Sister Geneviève of the Holy Face (Céline Martin), *My Sister Saint Thérèse*, authorized translation by the Carmelite Sisters of New York of Conseils et Souvenirs (Rockford, IL: Tan Books and Publishers, Inc., 1997), pp. 80–81.

8   John of Avila, *Certain Selected Spiritual Epistles* (Rouen: John Le Costurier, 1631), 35, p. 277.

9   John of the Cross, *The Spiritual Canticle* in *Collected Works*, translated by Kieran Kavanaugh and Otilio Rodriguez (Washington, D.C.: ICS Publications, 1991), Stanza 27, p. 519.

BIBLIOGRAPHY

Benedict XVI, Pope. *Apostolic Letter Proclaiming Saint John of Avila, diocesan priest, a Doctor of the Universal Church.* Vatican City: Libreria Editrice Vaticana, 2012.

_____. *Deus Caritas Est.* Vatican City: Libreria Editrice Vaticana, 2006.

_____. *Spe Salvi.* Vatican City: Libreria Editrice Vaticana, 2007.

Catechism of the Catholic Church. New York: Doubleday, 1995.

de la Palma, Luis. *The History of the Sacred Passion.* Translation Revised and Edited by Henry James Coleridge. London: Burns and Oates, 1875.

Dubay, Thomas. *Fire Within.* San Francisco: Ignatius Press, 1989.

Francis de Sales. *Introduction to the Devout Life.* Rockford, IL: Tan Books and Publishing, 2010.

_____. *Treatise on the Love of* God. Translated by Henry Benedict Mackey. Rockford, IL: Tan Books and Publishers, Inc., 1997.

Gabriel of St Mary Magdalen. *Divine Intimacy.* Translated from the 7th Italian Edition by the Discalced Carmelite Nuns of Boston. Published by Msgr Wm. J. Doheny, 1981.

Garrigou-Lagrange, Reginald. *Christian Perfection and Contemplation.* Translated by Sister M. Timothea Doyle. Rockford, IL: Tan Books and Publishers, Inc., 2003.

_____. *The Three Ages Of The Interior Life.* Volume I. Translated by Sister M. Timothea Doyle. Rockford, IL: Tan Books and Publishers, Inc., 1989.

Geneviève of the Holy Face, Sister (Céline Martin). *My Sister Saint Thérèse*. Authorized Translation by The Carmelite Sisters of New York of Conseils et Souvenirs. Rockford, IL: Tan Books and Publishers, Inc., 1997.

Hamling, Anna. 'John of Avila.' In *The Encyclopedia of Christian Literature*. Edited by George Thomas Kurian & James D. Smith, III. Vol. 1. Genres and Types/Biographies A-G. Lanham, MD: Scarecrow Press, Inc., 2010.

John of Avila. *Audi, Filia–Listen, O Daughter*. Translated and Introduced by Joan Frances Gormley. New York: Paulist Press, 2006.

_____. *Certain Selected Spiritual Epistles*. Rouen: John Le Costurier, 1631.

_____. *Letters of Blessed John of Avila*. Translated and Selected from the Spanish by the Benedictines of Stanbrook. London: Burns & Oates Ltd., 1904.

_____. *The Holy Ghost*. Translated by Ena Dargan. Dublin: Scepter Limited, 1959.

John of the Cross. *The Collected Works*. Translated by Kieran Kavanaugh and Otilio Rodriguez. Washington, D.C.: ICS Publications, 1991.

John Paul II, Pope. *Dives in Misericordia*. Boston: Pauline Books and Media, 1980.

Leo XIII, Pope. *Divinum Illud Munus*. http://www.vatican. va/holy_father/leo_xiii/encyclicals/documents/hf_l-xiii_enc_09051897_divinum-illud-munus_en.html, accessed 31 December 2012.

Marie-Eugène of the Child Jesus. *I Want to See God*. Vol. I. Translated by Sister M. Verda Clare. Notre Dame, IN: Christian Classics, 1998.

Martinez, Luis M. *The Sanctifier*. Translated by Sister M. Aquinas. Boston: Pauline Books and Media, 1985.

Oddi, Longaro degli. *Life of the Blessed Master John of Avila; Secular Priest, Called the Apostle of Andulusia.* London: Burns and Oates, 1898.

Peers, Edgar Allison. *The Mystics of Spain.* New York: Dover Publications, Inc., 2002.

Pinckaers, Servais. *The Sources of Christian Ethics.* Translated from the third edition by Sr Mary Thomas Noble. Edinburgh: T&T Clark, 1995.

Roldan-Figueroa, Rady. 'Espirituación: Juan de Ávila's Doctrine of Union with the Holy Spirit.' In *Renaissance and Reformation / Renaissance et Réforme.* Vol. XXIX, 2-3(2005): pp. 65–96.

Royo, Antonio and Jordan Aumann. *The Theology of Christian Perfection.* Dubuque, Iowa: The Priory Press, 1962.

Tanquerey, Adolphe. *The Spiritual life.* Translated by Herman Brandersis. New York: Desclee & Co., 1930.

Teresa of Avila. *The Collected Works.* Vol. I-II. Translated by Kieran Kavanaugh and Otilio Rodriguez. Washington, DC: ICS Publications, 1980.

_____. *The Letters of St Teresa.* Translated by John Dalton. London: Thomas Baker, 1902.

Thérèse of Lisieux. *Letters of St Thérèse of Lisieux, General Correspondence.* Vol. II. Translated from the Original Manuscripts by John Clarke. Washington, D.C.: ICS Publications, 1988.

_____. *Story of a Soul.* 3rd ed. Translated from the Original Manuscripts by John Clarke. Washington, D.C.: ICS Publications, 1996.

Thomas Aquinas. *Commentary by Saint Thomas Aquinas on the First Epistle to the Corinthians* Translated by Fabian Larcher (paragraphs 987-1046 translated by Daniel Keating). http://nvjournal.net/files/Aquinas-Corinthians.pdf, accessed May 21, 2012.

_____. *Commentary on the Gospel of St John*. Part I: Chapters 1-7. Translated by James A. Weisheipl. Albany, NY: Magi Books, Inc., 1998. http://dhspriory.org/thomas/ SSJohn.htm, accessed 21 May 2012.

_____. *Commentary on the Gospel of St John*. Part II: Chapters 8-21. Translated by Fabian R. Larcher. Albany, NY: Magi Books, Inc., 1998. http://dhspriory.org/thomas/ SSJohn.htm, accessed 21 May 2012.

_____. *The Light of Faith, The Compendium of Theology*. Translated by Cyril Vollert. Manchester, NH: Sophia Institute Press, 1993.

_____. *Summa Theologica*. Translated by the Fathers of the English Dominican Province. New York: Benziger Bros., 1948.

Tollemanche, Marguerite. *Spanish Mystics: A Sequel to Many Voices*. Whitefish, MT: Kessinger Publishing, 2005.

Vatican Council II. Lumen Gentium, Dogmatic Constitution on the Church. In Vatican Council II: The Conciliar and Post Conciliar Documents. Edited by Austin Flannery. New York: Costello Publishing Company, 1998.